Home-

SIMPLE HOUSEHOLD

REPAIRS

Peter Brooke-Ball

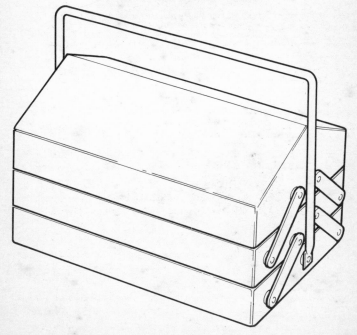

Ward Lock Limited · London

First published in Great Britain in 1988
by Ward Lock Limited, 8 Clifford Street,
London W1X 1RB, an Egmont Company.

Designed by Anita Ruddell

Illustrated by Simon Roulstone and Ivan Ripley
(pages 8, 10 (top), 33, 40, 42, 59, 71, 81, 84).

Text filmset in Baskerville No. 2
by MS Filmsetting Limited, Frome, Somerset
Printed and bound in Great Britain
by Richard Clay Ltd, Bungay, Suffolk

British Library Cataloguing in Publication Data
Brooke-Ball, Peter
  Simple household repairs.
  1. Residences. Maintenance & repair.
  Amateurs', Manuals
  I. Title   II. Series
  643'.7

  ISBN 0-7063-6673-5

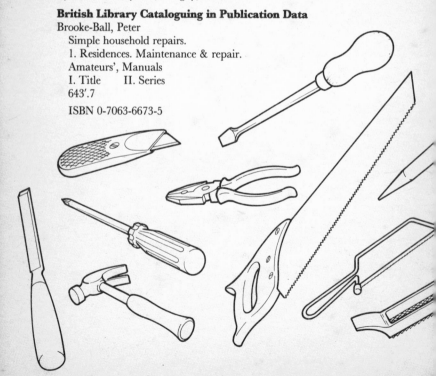

CONTENTS

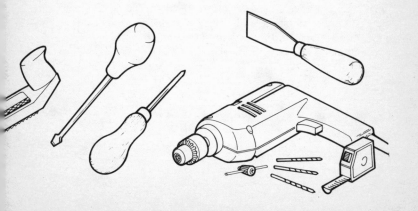

INTRODUCTION

No matter how well you organize and run your home, things are bound to go wrong or break from time to time – there is no way of predicting when a tap washer is going to perish or when a cup of coffee will be spilt on a carpet. No home is perfect and the purpose of this book is to show you how to put things right when they do go awry – everything from repairing a broken cup to clearing a blocked drain.

Correcting problems yourself will not only save you money, it can also save precious time. And you don't have to be a heavyweight DIY enthusiast or have any special knowledge to be successful. What you do need is a capable pair of hands, a few essential tools and a bit of know-how. This book provides the know-how in a way that is easy to follow, with no confusing jargon.

Before you start on a repair job, it sometimes helps to know how your home is put together and how services such as electricity and water work. For example, the water supply has to be turned off before you can repair a leaking tap and unless you know where the all-important cut-off tap is, you won't be able to start. A whole section is devoted to explaining how homes are constructed and details what you can and can't do yourself. If you don't think you can handle a job, don't risk it – it is far better to keep both you and your home intact.

Not all jobs are as straightforward as they appear – cleaning out a choked gutter seems simple enough, but you may not have a ladder or you may not have a head for heights. The obvious solutions to these snags is either to hire a ladder or to call in a professional. But this is sometimes easier said than done. Information in this book explains how to avoid 'cowboys' and get good value for money.

· 1 ·

GET TO KNOW YOUR HOUSE

Houses are like jigsaws – once you know how all the bits and pieces fit together, you have a clearer picture of how everything works. Pipes and wires can be particularly misleading and confusing because there sometimes seems to be no way of telling where they lead or what they serve. It makes sense to understand how the elements of a house slot together, as even with a minimal knowledge of your home's construction, you will be in a better position to tackle a fault when something goes wrong. Needless to say, building techniques have changed dramatically over the years, and plumbing and electricity arrangements have altered as well, but the basic essentials remain constant.

HOUSE CONSTRUCTION

All houses stand on foundations that are usually made from concrete and are sunk into the ground. The walls which stand on top of the foundations can be made of stone, wood and even mud, but most houses are built of brick. The walls in turn support the floors and roof.

☐ **Walls**

The *outside walls* on old houses are often solid brick. This makes them very sturdy but there is a chance that damp can work its way in from the outside. In modern houses, cavity walls are more common. With these, the walls have two 'leaves', the outer one made of brick and the inner one made of grey building blocks. The advantages of these walls is that they are cheaper and quicker to build, and the gap between the two leaves makes it more difficult for damp to penetrate to the inside of the house (fig. 1).

Interior walls can be either solid or hollow. Solid interior walls tend to be 'load-bearing', which means that they help to support the structure

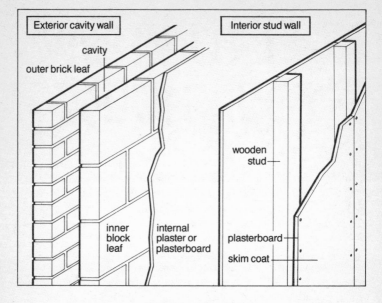

Fig. 1   *Wall types.*

of the house, while hollow walls, which are also called partition or stud walls, simply divide off areas into rooms and they do not support the ceiling above. Partition walls are made by nailing sheets of plasterboard to vertical timber 'studs' which are fixed to the floor and ceiling. You can tell if a wall is hollow by tapping it with your knuckles. Plasterboard can be decorated without applying a plaster coat first, but in most cases a thin 'skim' of plaster is applied to give a uniform finish. Most solid interior walls are plastered to provide a smooth surface for decoration.

☐ Floors

There are two main types of floor: solid and timber. The ground floor of a house is usually solid. Solid floors are made out of concrete which is laid over a sheet of plastic to keep out the damp from the ground.

Timber floors, which are also called suspended floors, are built on top of wooden joists that are supported by the walls. Floorboards are nailed on top of the joists and sheets of plasterboard or lath and plaster are fixed to the underside (fig. 2).

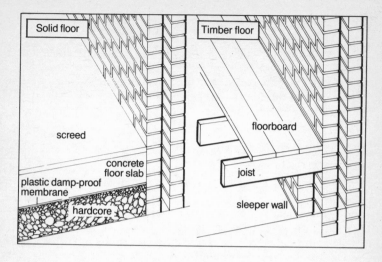

Fig 2 *Floor types.*

☐ **Roofs**

A frame of wooden rafters support the roof. Frames come in many different shapes and sizes and they are fixed to the tops of the walls. Slates and tiles are the most common roofing materials and they are both fixed with nails to battens, which run across the rafters (fig. 3).

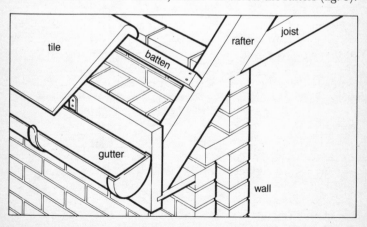

Fig. 3 *Roofing materials.*

SERVICES

The essential services such as water, electricity, drainage and gas are often taken for granted. Until, that is, something goes wrong. Not every house is connected to a main gas supply or to a public sewer system (in rural areas cesspools or septic tanks take care of waste water) but they are common to most town dwellers.

☐ The electricity supply

Electricity enters most homes via an underground service cable which is thick and black. The usual place to find this cable is under the stairs or in the hallway. The service cable ends at a black service fusebox and from here two black cables lead to the meter. The service cable, service fuse and meter are the property of the Electricity Board and they should not be tampered with. From the meter, cables run to the main fusebox and to the various outlets which supply electricity to the circuits (fig. 4). A special yellow and green wire runs from the fusebox to an earthing point which is usually a pipe.

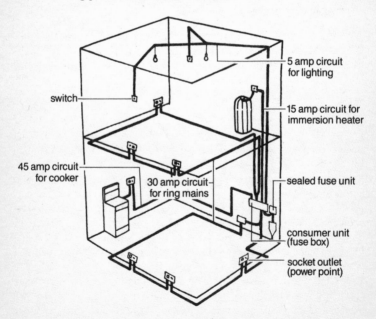

Fig. 4 *The electricity circuit.*

Each circuit in a house is protected by a fuse – a deliberate weak link which 'blows' if the circuit is overloaded. There are four common types of fuse:

- 5 amp (white) for lighting circuits
- 15 amp (blue) for an immersion heater
- 30 amp (red) for power (plug) circuits
- 45 amp (green) for large cookers or heating equipment.

The main switch for turning off the electricity supply is also sighted in or near the fusebox.

From the fusebox, cables run around the house to feed outlet points. It is common to find two lighting circuits – one for upstairs and one for downstairs – and two power circuits.

Cables run under floorboards, behind skirting boards and up walls. It is never easy to trace them because it means lifting up carpets and hammering into walls. The important thing to remember is that if you notice any old or tatty cables, especially ones sheathed in rubber, they could be dangerous and it may be worth having the house rewired.

☐ **The water supply**

The average house receives its water via an underground pipe which comes up in the kitchen or under the stairs. This pipe is called the rising main and it runs straight up through the house to the cold water storage cistern in the loft, which it feeds through a ball valve. It is usual to find that the kitchen tap is connected directly to the rising main but all the other cold taps and WCs are supplied with water from the storage cistern. The cistern also keeps the hot water cylinder full of water. The water in the hot water cylinder is either heated by a boiler or by an immersion heater and is piped around a separate circuit to all the hot taps (fig. 5).

Stopcocks are fitted to pipes which supply water under pressure and are found on the rising main – there is usually one under the sink and this is the one that should be turned off in an emergency. Gate valves are sited on low-pressure pipes and you usually find them on the draw-off pipes from the cold water storage cistern. These are often the first line of defence if you want to isolate a part of the water system, so it is worth finding out where yours are (fig. 6).

Some houses have what is called a *direct* water system where all the cold taps and WCs are fed from the rising main. These systems are frowned upon by many water authorities and they can be noisy because all the water is under pressure.

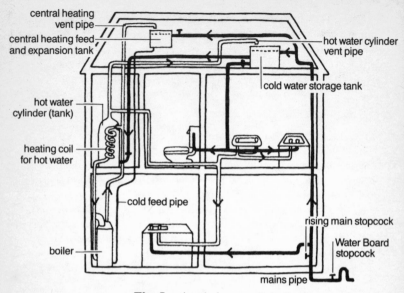

Fig. 5 *A typical water supply.*

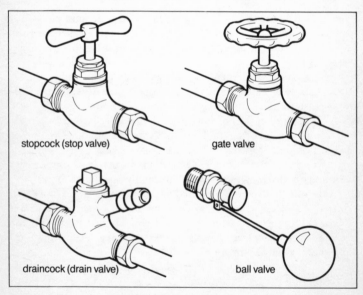

Fig. 6 *Different types of valve.*

Central heating systems usually have a separate circuit to the hot water supply so that the tapwater is not contaminated.

Water pipes are found under floorboards and buried inside walls which can make them difficult to trace. It is also easy to confuse central heating pipes with hot water ones – the usual trick to find out which is which is to turn on the heating and to determine which pipes become hot.

☐ **Drainage systems**

There are three categories of drainage water: waste water comes from sinks and baths, foul water comes from WCs and rainwater comes from gutters. All three types have to be channelled away safely so that they don't pollute or contaminate clean water or the surrounding area. There are two common types of drainage system found.

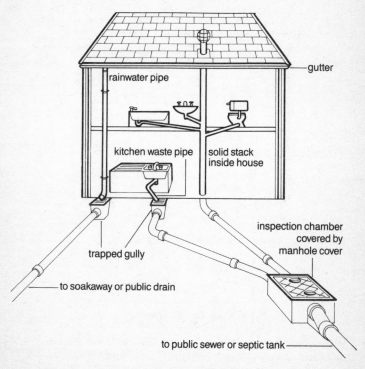

Fig. 7 *A one-pipe drainage system.*

In a *two-pipe system*, foul water flows into a soil pipe that leads directly to an inspection chamber which is covered with a manhole cover. Waste water runs into a downpipe which is often topped with a 'hopper' head. This water flows to an outside gulley and is then ducted underground to the inspection chamber. Rainwater runs down pipes which lead to gulleys and from there it goes to an underground 'soakaway' or to a public drain.

In a *one-pipe system*, which is more common on modern houses, a vertical soil pipe collects both foul and waste water (fig. 7). Waste from the kitchen sink is sometimes dealt with separately.

□ The gas supply

Gas is another service that is ducted to houses underground. Meters can be sited both inside and outside the house and should not be tampered with at any cost. Beside the meter there is a main gas tap which cuts off the supply – if you smell gas around the house and can't find out where it comes from, this is the tap to turn off (fig. 8).

From the meter, the gas is ducted to outlet points around the house, such as fires, cookers and boilers. Most gas appliances are connected to the supply pipes with special fittings that have to be dealt with by a qualified gas fitter – on no account try to fix a fault by yourself.

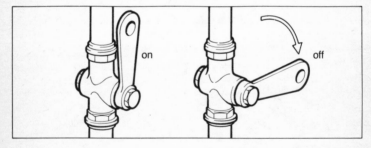

Fig. 8 *A gas tap.*

DIY OR HIRING HELP?

The first question you should ask yourself before tackling a repair job is 'Am I taking a risk?'. If you have any doubts, then it is foolhardy to go ahead. Of course, sometimes a risk isn't always obvious. For example, replacing a pendant light bulb is straightforward enough, but climbing

DIY or Hiring Help?

a stepladder to reach it doesn't suit everybody and it is only too easy to topple off. Think twice before you start.

Jobs you should not do yourself unless you are an expert include:

● gas repairs
● electricity repairs to mains cables or circuits
● structural alterations.

If you want to get in expert help, there is a right and wrong way to go about it. Above all, be wary of 'cowboy' tradesmen who offer cheap prices but no qualifications or guarantees.

☐ Qualifications to look for

A tradesman or builder who has been recommended by a friend is often worth hiring because at least you will have an idea of the quality of his work. But it is worth looking out for specific qualifications as well. Many plumbers, builders and electricians advertise in *Yellow Pages* and list their qualifications alongside their names. The following recognized guilds or associations give stamps of approval:

● The Federation of Master Builders (for general builders, plumbers, damp and roofing specialists)
● The Guild of Master Craftsmen (for carpenters and joiners)
● The Institute of Plumbing (for plumbers)
● The Confederation of Registered Gas Installers – CORGI (for heating engineers, plumbers and gas fitters)
● National Inspection Council for Electrical Installation Contracting – NICEIC (for electricians)
● British Pest Control Association – BPCA (for pest control specialists)
● British Wood Preserving Association (for specialists in rot, woodworm and damp)
● Royal Institute of British Architects – RIBA (for architects).

☐ Quotes and estimates

Before hiring a professional, it is worth getting quotes for the job in hand from several different people. This will enable you to compare prices. Most professionals give quotes free of charge, so you don't lose out in any way.

A quote is a definite price for a job and should include a list of all the details. It means that the person will do the job as laid out provided he is contracted to do so within a specified time. If, at the end of the day, the job costs more, that is not your problem. When you ask for a quote, make sure that it is written down on paper and check that all the details of the job are included and that you understand what is to be done.

A quote should not be confused with an estimate, which is not legally binding in any way – this is purely an estimate for a job and the final cost could come out above or under the figure.

☐ **What to expect**

If you have hired a qualified person, you can expect high-quality work. If it turns out to be shoddy or defective, your best bet is to contact the body that issued the qualification. They will advise you further and be able to tell you what your next step should be. Professional builders invariably take longer than they originally stated. Unfortunately there is not much anyone can realistically do about this except hang on.

HOME IMPROVEMENT GRANTS

If you have major improvements to carry out, you may be able to get a council grant to help pay for the cost. In England and Wales (Scotland has its own system) there are four main types of grant. If you think you are eligible, contact your council's Grant Officer. Some grants are mandatory, meaning that they have to be given, others are discretionary and are only awarded as and when the council sees fit. Amounts can vary from area to area so there are no hard and fast rules.

When you apply for a grant, you will have to fill out a suitable form and you will also be asked to supply a valid quote for the job. Once your application has been submitted and accepted (this can take several months), you can get the work done, pay for it, and then be reimbursed by the council.

Improvement grants are meant to help pay for the cost of a major improvement such as rewiring or putting in a damp-proof course. They are discretionary and are not always awarded.

Repair grants are given where structural repairs are essential to a house built before 1919. They are discretionary and are given for such projects as reroofing or repairing damaged foundations.

Intermediate grants are mandatory but they can only be applied for if you don't have an essential amenity such as a bath, a WC or a hot water system.

Insulation grants are discretionary and are designed to help pay for the lagging of lofts, pipes and hot water cylinders.

·2·

TOOLS & MATERIALS

You don't need many tools or special materials to carry out repairs in and around the home and you almost certainly won't need everything that is listed below. It's much more likely that you will buy items as and when you need them. Some tools and materials are sold in kits or packs. There is nothing wrong with buying equipment like this but ultimately you end up paying for the packaging as well.

USEFUL MATERIALS

It is worth keeping a small stock of assorted screws and nails, some adhesive and a roll or two of tape, as these will always get used up.

Nails are usually sold by weight but if you don't want a large quantity, you can also get them in packs: 25 mm (1 in) and 50 mm (2 in) wire nails are the sorts most frequently used. A selection of panel pins is also worth having.

Screws are sold by the box or in packs but often the first decision is to choose between *crosshead* and *slot head* types. Most sizes are available in both styles, so choose types that match your screwdrivers. As well as coming in a variety of lengths, screws also vary in girth which is measured by a gauge number – 4 gauge is the smallest and 12 gauge the largest. For most uses No 8 screws are adequate. If you are fixing into walls, you will probably need to get *plugs* as well. Make sure you buy a type and size that is compatible with the screws you are using – if you are in doubt consult the retailer or study the back of the packet.

Clear tape and masking tape are frequently used for a hundred and one different jobs. Masking tape is invaluable if you are touching up paintwork or don't want to mark a surface. *Carpet tapes* are stronger and are useful if you want to make a semi-permanent repair to furnishings or floor coverings.

Nails	Description	Used for	Sizes
Round	Large head; circular in cross-section	Fixing wood to wood	19–150 mm ($\frac{3}{4}$–6 in)
Oval	Small head; oval in cross-section	Fixing wood to wood (less likely to split timber)	25–150 mm (1–6 in)
Flooring brad	Lopsided head; rectangular in cross-section	Fixing floorboards	25–150 mm (1–6 in)
Lost-head	Tiny head; round cross-section	Fixing wood to wood (head becomes invisible)	25–150 mm (1–6 in)
Panel pin	Tiny head; small thickness	Cabinet making and for fixing mouldings	16–50 mm ($\frac{5}{8}$–2 in)

Type	Description	Use	Size
Clout	Large head; galvanized shank	Fixing sash cords and roofing felt	19–50 mm ($\frac{3}{4}$–2 in)
Plasterboard	Large head; rough, galvanized shank	Fixing plasterboard sheets	25–50 mm (1–2 in)
Tack	Sharp point; relatively large head	Securing carpets and fabrics	6–31 mm ($\frac{1}{4}$–1$\frac{1}{4}$ in)
Sprig	No head; angled shank	Glazing windows	12–19 mm ($\frac{1}{2}$–$\frac{3}{4}$ in)
Masonry	Small head; toughened steel	Fixing to masonry	25–100 mm (1–4 in)
Annular	Large head; rings on shank	Fixing sheet materials to wood (the rings grip the timber)	19–100 mm ($\frac{3}{4}$–4 in)

Screws	Description	Used for	Lengths
Countersunk	Flat head which is designed to lie flush with the surface	Fixing countersunk wood or fittings to wood or masonry (with wallplug)	12–100 mm ($\frac{1}{2}$–4 in)
Round head	Hemispherical head which is designed to lie on top of surface	Fixing fittings without countersunk holes to wood or masonry (with wallplug)	12–50 mm ($\frac{1}{2}$–2 in)
Raised head	Slightly curved head which is partly sunk into surface	Fixing specially designed fittings to wood	12–50 mm ($\frac{1}{2}$–2 in)
Dome head	Two-part screw – dome is fixed into head	Fixing mirrors to walls (the dome is screwed on to hide the screw head)	25–50 mm (1–2 in)
Chipboard	Countersunk head; deep cutting threads	Fixing chipboard panels	25–50 mm (1–2 in)
Special	Screw eyes and hooks	Hanging things on wooden panels or walls	various

Epoxy adhesive is immensely strong and can be used to mend just about anything. However it sets slowly, so a quick setting *superglue* is always worth having. Glues for special surfaces are best bought when needed.

☐ Paint and papers

Household paint is sold in cans – if you are given a choice between a metal or plastic can, choose the plastic type as they don't rust and therefore won't contaminate any paint that is left over to store. Most of the types of paint listed in the chart (on pp. 22–3) are sold in 1L, 2.5L or 5L cans but if you are touching up emulsion paint, consider buying a 'sampler' bottle. These are available in a number of shades and they will save you the expense of buying a whole can.

Before storing paint, clean up the rim of the lid so that there is no dried paint on it that could fall into the fresh paint. Push the lid right on to form an airtight seal and then keep the can upside down in a dry place; by placing the can upside down, the scum that will inevitably form on the paint will be at the bottom when you reopen the can.

It is extremely hard to match new wallpaper to old wallpaper, and even if you do manage to get the same pattern, the colours may be slightly different. The moral is to keep any offcuts of wallpaper after a room has been redecorated. You can then use these for repairs.

☐ Abrasive papers

Abrasive papers are often called sandpapers although this is not technically correct. Abrasive papers are graded according to the grit size (fine, medium and coarse) and also by number, which refers to the density of the grit on the sheet. The commonest type of abrasive paper is *glasspaper*, which is suitable for sanding down timber. Use coarse glasspaper to smooth down rough wood and fine glasspaper to finish it off. Flour paper is the finest glasspaper of all and gives a glassy finish. The other type of abrasive paper is called *silicon-carbide paper* or *wet and dry*. As its name implies, it can be used dry or with water – water acts as a lubricant and makes the abrasive more efficient. Wet and dry can be used on gloss paints and on steel.

☐ Oils

A *light engineering oil* is suitable for most jobs but you may prefer to get a *graphite oil* for extra lubrication, or a *penetrating oil* if you want to free something that is well and truly jammed.

Adhesives	Suitable for	Solvent (cleaner) NB *always refer to container if in doubt*	Notes
Animal glue	Wood	Water	Seldom used but very strong
PVA	Wood, fabrics, paper, leather	Water	Not waterproof; easy to use
Contact	Fabrics, paper, laminates, leather	Nail varnish remover (acetone)	Flexible but not very strong; gives off inflammable fumes
Clear	Wood, pottery, plastics, leather	Nail varnish remover (acetone)	Flexible; not very strong; relatively expensive (sold in tubes); for general purpose use only
Superglue	Wood, pottery, paper, leather, plastics, china, metal	Nail varnish remover (acetone) or special superglue remover	Expensive general purpose glue; quick setting; potentially dangerous (have a special super-glue remover to hand)
Latex	Fabrics, leather, paper	Water	Flexible and waterproof

Urea formaldehyde	Wood	Soapy water	Outdoor wood adhesive; waterproof
Vinyl cement	Vinyl (PVC)	Nail varnish remover (acetone)	Strong and flexible; 'welds' sheets together
Epoxy	Wood, fabrics, leather, pottery, china, plastics, metal	White spirit	Hardener and adhesive mixed together; very strong; waterproof
Glue gun	Wood, fabrics, leather, laminates, pottery, china, plastics, metal	White spirit/nail varnish remover (acetone)	Various glues available for use with guns; expensive
Wallpaper paste	Wallpaper	Water	Can be used to make papier mâché
Glue sticks	Paper	Water/white spirit	Easy to use; weak bond; suitable for general purpose only
Acrylic cement	Acrylic sheeting	Nail varnish remover (acetone)	Gives off noxious fumes

Paints	Choice	Uses/qualities
Primers	Universal primer	Oil-based; can be used on wood, metal and plaster
	Wood primer	Oil-based; used to prime bare wood (avoid types which contain lead)
	Aluminium primer	Oil-based; used to prime hardwoods and stripped timber; also used to seal plaster
	Zinc chromate primer	Used on bare metals of all kinds
Preparatory sealers	Knotting	Used to seal weeping knots in softwood prior to priming
	Stabilizing fluid	Used to seal flaking masonry before painting
Undercoats	Oil-based undercoat	Used on wood and plaster as a two-in-one primer and undercoat; wood needs sanding after application
	Water-based undercoat	Available in several shades to match topcoat; good covering power; used on wood and metal
Topcoats (oil-based)	Alkyd resin paint	A type of oil-based paint; can be used indoors or out; special undercoat may be required; available in matt or gloss

Polyurethane resin paint	Available in liquid and non-drip forms in a vast range of colours; can be used on wood or metal; usually gloss; hardwearing and water-resistant (non-drip requires no undercoat)
Topcoats (water-based) — Interior emulsion	Available in gloss, semi-gloss and matt finishes; comes in liquid, non-drip and 'solid' forms; can be brushed or rolled; suitable for wood, paper and plaster
Exterior emulsion	Hardwearing, water-resistant and not affected by ultra-violet rays; can be rolled or brushed; for use on masonry
Microporous paint	For use on bare wood outside; allows timber to breathe; quick drying
Special paints — Bituminous paint	A black or brown paint used to waterproof gutters, downpipes and walls; cannot be painted over
Enamel paint	Relatively expensive; used on clean metal or wood; does not require primer or undercoat; best used in small quantities; gives a high gloss
Lacquer paint	Gives similar finish to enamel but is solvent-based; can be used on wood or metal; available in aerosol cans
Anti-condensation paint	Emulsions suitable for use in kitchens and bathrooms; insulates surface and absorbs moisture; will not cure condensation

☐ **Solvents**

White spirit is the most frequently used solvent – it can be used to lift paint and oil stains. *Methylated spirits* is another solvent worth having around and is especially useful for cleaning glass and metal. *Acetone* is not an everyday solvent, but it is about the only thing that will dissolve certain glues. It gives off noxious fumes so should only be used in well-ventilated spaces.

☐ **Fillers**

Cellulose fillers come either as powder that you mix with water, or as a ready-mixed paste – there is little difference between the two forms, except that powder is usually cheaper. These fillers are adequate for filling holes in plaster or wood but if you want to use them outside, make sure you get an exterior-quality type. Regardless of what they say on the packets, cellulose fillers do tend to crack, especially if they are laid on thickly. Once they have been sanded down, they can, and should, be decorated over.

Epoxy fillers are more expensive and they take longer to set, but they are tougher than cellulose types. They come in two parts that have to be mixed together and there are special types for filling metal and wood.

GENERAL TOOLKIT

There are no hard and fast rules about what should or shouldn't be in a toolkit – in most cases, toolkits grow as more tools are added over the years. However, the following tend to be used frequently (fig. 9).

A trimming or *handyman's knife* is essential. They have sharp, replaceable blades and can be used for countless different jobs. The sort which enable you to withdraw the blade are a good buy.

A hammer of some description is invaluable. A claw hammer enables old nails to be withdrawn easily, but they can be heavy so try wielding one before you make a choice. The alternative to a claw hammer is a pin hammer, which is lighter and has a small head. These are useful for knocking in pins and small nails.

Screwdrivers in various sizes are useful. A small screwdriver will not be adequate for a large screw, and a large screwdriver will most likely damage a small screw. It is also a good idea to have at least one *crosshead* screwdriver and one *slot head* screwdriver. Try to avoid kits which

▶ *Tools & Materials*

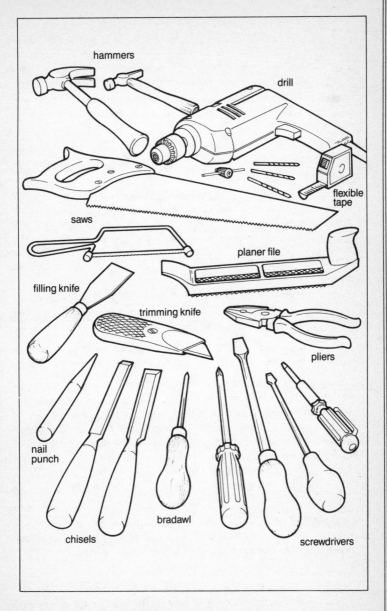

Fig. 9 *Frequently used tools.*

enable you to exchange sizes and types of screwdriver – they tend to be made from weak metal. Ideally, large screwdrivers should have oval rather than round handles, which makes them easier to use. An *electrician's* screwdriver is useful for testing sockets and for wiring plugs, but make sure that the insulation goes right down to the end of the tip.

A bradawl is handy for starting holes in timber or plaster. They are inexpensive and well worth having; they can even be used as small screwdrivers.

A steel tape is well worth the money; it is usually unnecessary to get a type which locks the rule. The alternative is a rigid steel ruler but these tend to go rusty after a while.

An adjustable spanner is essential for plumbing work and you may in fact need two. Get a sort with jaws that open at least 25 mm (1 in) wide and be wary of cheap ones.

Chisels are not essential but it is sometimes useful to have an old one around that you can use for scraping and levering. An option is to buy a special scraper with a stiff blade.

Saws can be expensive so choose wisely. A small *panel saw* is adequate for most repair and household jobs. You will need a *junior hacksaw* if you want to cut through metal, such as pipes.

A planer file is the poor man's plane but they are easier to use and are much less expensive. A selection of shapes and blade types is available.

An electric drill is a must. Unless you are going to use it a lot, get an ordinary two-speed type with a 12 mm ($\frac{1}{2}$ in) chuck. Various accessories can be added to a drill, including sanding discs and jigsaws. In order to use the drill, you will need a selection of high speed *wood bits* and possibly a couple of *masonry bits* as well if you intend to drill into brickwork or concrete (masonry bits have spade-shaped tips that are made out of toughened steel). A *countersink* is another good drill attachment that will allow you to sink screws below the surface of wood.

A nail punch is often considered a specialist tool but it is, in fact, frequently needed when you want to hammer a nail head below the surface. However, they are relatively expensive and you may be able to improvise with an old screwdriver.

A flexible filling knife is useful for patching jobs. Buy a good quality knife with a really flexible blade – you'll find that the extra cost is money well spent.

A pair of pliers should always be included in a toolkit. You can use them for lifting out screws and nails as well as for bending wires and strips of metal. Get a blunt-nosed type with serrated jaws that enable you to get a good grip.

TIPS ON USING TOOLS

To help you make your repairs more effective and easier to do, here are some hints.

Drilling   When drilling holes in wood turn the speed on your drill to slow so that the fibres aren't torn. When drilling metal or masonry, mark a start hole first so that the bit doesn't slip, and use a high speed on the drill.

Sawing   If the blade sticks while you are sawing a piece of timber, rub some candle wax over the blade to lubricate it.

Hammering   Hammering sounds simple but many people hold the shaft too high up and then complain that the nails bend over. This is a sign that the hammer is too heavy, so use a lighter type. To prevent nails bending over, it sometimes helps if you angle the nails into the timber; this also guarantees a firmer fixing.

Screwing   If you are screwing into wood, it is best to drill a pilot hole for the screw threads, a clearance hole for the shaft and a countersunk hole for the head (fig. 10). This sounds laborious but it guarantees that the wood won't split and that you end up with a good finish.

Sanding   You get a better, more even finish when sanding if you wrap the abrasive paper round a block of wood. If you are smoothing down a curved surface, you can improvise a suitably shaped block from things like an old broom handle.

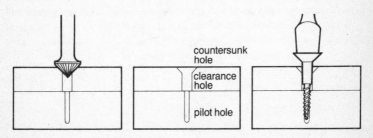

Fig. 10   *Types of screw hole.*

◀ Tools & Materials

·3·
EMERGENCY REPAIRS

When something drastic goes wrong in your house – your main fuse blows, a ball is accidentally kicked through your front window, a waste pipe becomes blocked, or your roof develops a leak – emergency repairs need to be undertaken without delay. This chapter deals with these sorts of situations and explains how you can cope.

CHANGING FUSES

Fuses are deliberately weak links in electrical circuits that are designed to protect rather than hinder (fig. 11). If something goes wrong in a circuit or appliance – overloading or a short circuit, for example – the fuse blows before the appliance or wiring system. Fuses are found in plugs and in the consumer unit (fusebox) which is often hidden in a cupboard under the stairs. If you have an appliance or system that persistently blows a fuse, call in a qualified electrician to have a look at the problem.

☐ Replacing a plug fuse

If an electrical appliance suddenly stops working for no apparent reason, the plug fuse may have blown. This is sometimes accompanied by a pop from the plug. Renewing a plug fuse is comparatively simple provided you have a suitable replacement. The first thing to do is check that the replacement fuse is of the correct rating for the appliance, in most cases either 3 amp or 13 amp: 3 amp fuses are for appliances such as table lamps, televisions and radios; 13 amp fuses are required for appliances such as electric fires, power tools and food mixers. If you are in doubt about the correct fuse rating, ask an electrician, the manufacturer of the appliance or any Electricity Board shop.

Fig. 11
Types of fuse.

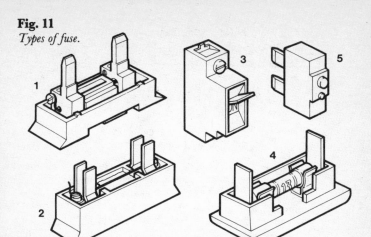

1. *Single-bladed carrier with wire fuse.*
2. *Double-bladed carrier with wire fuse.*
3. *Switch-operated miniature circuit breaker.*
4. *Cartridge fuse carrier.*
5. *Button-operated miniature circuit breaker.*

To renew a plug fuse:

1 Unscrew the cover on the plug and lever out the blown fuse with a small screwdriver.

2 Check that all the wires are firmly fixed in their terminals and that there are no strands of flex visible.

3 Push the new fuse into place and replace the cover.

☐ Repairing a blown main fuse

You will know when a main fuse goes because a whole series of lights or plugs will suddenly cease to work. Changing a fuse in a fusebox (more properly called a consumer unit) is easy provided you know what type of fusebox you are dealing with and have an appropriate repair kit.

Before attempting to mend or change the fuse, turn off the electricity supply at the mains switch which is usually located adjacent to the consumer unit. After you have switched off, you can safely attend the fuses (fig. 12).

Rewirable fuse Before you can mend a rewirable fuse, you will need a small electrician's screwdriver, a torch and a length of appropriate fuse

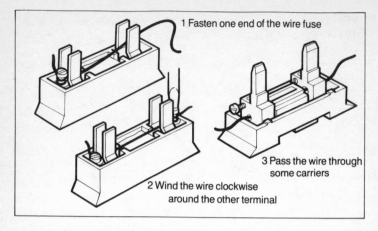

Fig. 12 *Rewiring a fuse.*

wire. Fuse wire comes in four main thicknesses for 5 amp, 15 amp, 30 amp and 45 amp circuits. Make sure you use a length of wire that matches the amp rating stamped on the fuse holder. To mend the fuse:

1 With the electricity turned off, pull out the fuse holder with the blown fuse. It is not always easy to tell which fuse has blown so you may have to check all the fuse holders until you find the right one.

2 Using the small screwdriver, loosen the screws at either end of the fuse holder which holds the wire in place. Pull out any strands of wire which remain.

3 Cut a length of wire long enough to straddle the gap between the two securing screws. Fix the wire in place by winding it clockwise around the screws, which can then be tightened up.

4 Replace the fuse holder and switch on at the mains.

Cartridge fuse In order to change a blown cartridge fuse, you will need a matching replacement, a torch and an electrician's screwdriver:

1 Turn off the electricity at the mains and locate the blown fuse by pulling out each fuse holder in turn. With most cartridge fuse holders you have to unscrew the two halves in order to gain access to the cartridge inside. You will be able to identify the damaged fuse because it will be blackened and charred.

2 Prise out the old fuse and replace it with a new one. Screw the two halves of the fuse holder back together again and replace it in the consumer unit.

3 Turn the electricity back on at the mains.

Miniature circuit breakers serve the same function as traditional fuses but they don't actually blow as such – they 'trip' instead, and they need only to be reset:

1 Turn off the electricity at the mains and identify the tripped circuit breaker. Identification is simple because the red button at the top will have popped out.

2 Press the button in – this will reset the circuit breaker.

3 Turn the electricity supply back on at the mains.

Emergency electrical toolkit

A small collection of essential tools and materials, kept near the consumer unit (fusebox) can save a lot of time and trouble should a fuse blow. The kit should contain the following:

● a torch
● a selection of 3 amp and 13 amp plug fuses
● an electrician's screwdriver
● spare fuse wire or fuse cartridges, as appropriate (miniature circuit breakers do not need any replacement parts).

CHANGING LIGHT BULBS

All light bulbs eventually burn out with age, so it isn't necessarily an indication that something is wrong with the circuit when a light bulb burns out. Before replacing a blown light bulb, check that the new one has a suitable wattage – some table lamps for example, should not be fitted with bulbs exceeding 60 watts.

☐ Bayonet light bulbs

These are the most common sort in domestic use and they are straightforward to change:

1 Switch off the light before removing the blown bulb. With a two-way circuit like those found in some hallways, play safe by turning the electricity off at the mains.

2 Allow the bulb to cool before attempting to remove it, and protect your hands by wearing gloves or by smothering the bulb in a cloth. Do not attempt to remove a hot bulb using a wet rag as this may cause the bulb to explode. Remove the bulb by pushing it into the lamp holder and twisting it anti-clockwise.

3 Insert the new bulb into the holder and fix it in place by pushing it into the holder and twisting it clockwise.

☐ **Screw-fit bulb**

Replacing a screw-fit bulb is easily done. Simply turn off the switch, unscrew the old bulb and screw in a new one.

☐ **Fluorescent tube**

If a fluorescent tube begins to flicker it could be that the tube needs replacing or, alternatively, the starter may be faulty (see below). If the light from the tube begins to dull, the chances are that it needs replacing. Always handle fluorescent tubes with care – they tend to implode rather than explode and the glass is extremely thin and fragile. To replace a tube:

1 Turn off the light switch and then, at one end of the tube, pull the spring-loaded bracket outwards. This will release the two connecting pins which hold the tube in place. With one end of the tube free, you will be able to pull the tube out of the other bracket.

2 Fit the new tube by reversing the process, making sure that the pins at each end engage in the brackets.

Fluorescent tube starters are cylindrical plugs which fit directly into the side or top of fluorescent tube lamp holders. To replace a starter:

1 After switching off, remove the starter by twisting it anti-clockwise.

2 Fit a new starter by reversing the procedure, making sure that the lugs fit into their slots.

REPLACING A BROKEN WINDOW PANE

The procedure for fitting a new sheet of glass into a window is much the same regardless of whether the frame is made of wood or metal (fig. 13). You will need glazier's putty, new glass, 12 mm ($\frac{1}{2}$ in) glazing sprigs (or glazing clips for a metal window), touching-up paint, a putty or filling knife, an old chisel or screwdriver, a pair of pliers, a tape measure and a thick pair of gloves:

1 Wearing gloves, lift out as much of the broken glass as possible; use pliers to remove small shards. Wrap the glass in several layers of newspaper before putting it in the bin. Rake out the old putty with a chisel and pull out glazing sprigs or pins with your pliers. With the putty out of the way, brush down the rebate (the angle into which the pane fits) to get rid of dust and dirt.

2 Take the inside measurements of the rebate and then subtract 3 mm ($\frac{1}{8}$ in) from your figures so that when the new pane is cut to the

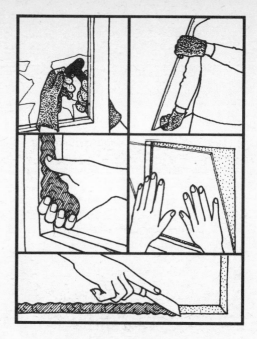

Fig. 13 *Replacing a broken window.*

smaller measurements, it will fit freely. Have the new pane of glass cut for you buy a professional glazier. Take a fragment of the old pane with you to the glazier so that the thickness can be matched.

3   Roll out a 'sausage' of well-mixed putty and mould this into the rebate. The putty in the rebate should be about 6 mm ($\frac{1}{4}$ in) thick.

4   Position the new pane in the rebate and press it into the putty which should squeeze out all round. If you are dealing with a wooden frame, fix the glass in position by tapping in glazing sprigs spaced out at 15 cm (6 in) intervals. It is easiest if you use the edge of a chisel to tap in the sprigs. If the frame is metal, use clips to secure the pane.

5   Apply another 'sausage' of putty to the edges of the glass and smooth this into a neat angle which you can copy from adjacent windows. If putty sticks to the knife, dip it in water. Remove excess putty from inside using your putty knife and then wipe off finger prints on the glass with a rag dipped in methylated spirits.

6   Leave the putty for a couple of weeks or so to harden up and then paint over it; ideally, the paint should overlap the putty on to the glass by about 3 mm ($\frac{1}{8}$ in) so that it creates a watertight seal.

CLEARING BLOCKED DRAINS AND SINKS

Nobody likes clearing drains but the job should be done as quickly as possible before bacteria begin to breed and the smells become unbearable.

□ Clearing sink, bath and basin waste pipes

All sinks, baths and basins have traps directly underneath the outlets that are designed to catch solid matter which could block the pipes further down the run (fig. 14). It is in traps that most blockages are found. There are five common types of trap.

If, after cleaning the trap, the blockage remains, it is best to call in a plumber: blockages in pipework are not so easy to clear and it is more than likely that you will consolidate and compress the debris if you start pushing down rods and wires.

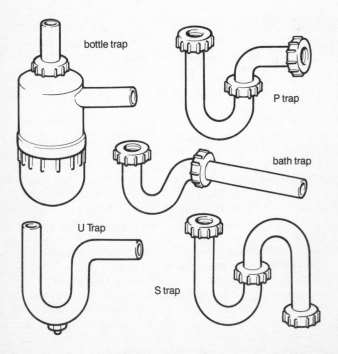

Fig. 14 *Different trap types.*

Bottle trap   To gain direct access to the blockage inside a bottle trap, follow this procedure:

1   Bale out as much of the water as possible from the basin or sink with an old mug.

2   Place a bowl under the trap to catch any drips.

3   Unscrew the base section of the trap and pull out any debris.

4   Make sure the two pipes inside the trap are clean before screwing the base back in place.

P-traps and S-traps   These are very similar in design – they are both made of plastic and the U-section has to be removed in order to get at the blockage:

1   Empty as much water as you can from the basin or sink.

2   Position a bucket or bowl under the trap and unscrew the plastic nuts which hold the U-section in place.

3   With the U-section removed, pull out any debris with a bent wire coat hanger and flush out the pipe.

4   Replace the U-section, making sure that you don't leave out any of the sealing washers.

U-traps   These are invariably made of metal that has corroded. This obviously makes them a bit more tricky to clear:

1   Place a bowl under the trap to catch the debris and water.

2   Locate the clearing eye which is at the very bottom of the bend. It is unlikely that you will be able to unscrew this by hand and you will probably need an old screwdriver. Slot the screwdriver between the lugs and turn it anti-clockwise. Try not to distort or twist the piping as you do this.

3   Pull out the blockage with a stout piece of wire and then replace the clearing eye stopper.

Bath traps   These are like shallow P-traps. They are invariably hidden from view behind panelling and it is usually easiest to tackle the problem through the outlet. To do this you will need a flexible cleaning wire with a 'screw' on the end. These are quite cheap and are readily available from hardware shops. Try to avoid using such chemicals as caustic soda as they are potentially dangerous and may ruin the surface on your bath. To clear a bath trap:

1   Remove hair and any matted material from around the outlet, then insert the clearing wire, twisting it as you push it in. The screw on the wire will catch the blockage which can then be pulled out.

2   Repeat the process until you are certain that the blockage has gone, then run the taps to flush out the pipes.

▶ *Emergency Repairs*

□ **Clearing a blocked WC**

Nearly all WC blockages occur in the trap behind the pan. To clear this you will need a special plunger which is larger than the ordinary type. You should be able to hire one but if you can't, you can try wrapping a polythene bag around a mop and using this instead. To clear the trap:

1 Place the plunger over the outlet in the pan and move it up and down rapidly a dozen or so times. This should release the blockage and the waste will gurgle away.

2 Flush the cistern a couple of times to clear out the system.

□ **Clearing main drains**

This can be a mucky, smelly and time-consuming business. It may also need more than one person if you have to remove a manhole cover. For this reason, your best bet is to call in a specialist drain clearing company. Such companies are listed under Drains in *Yellow Pages*.

Gas leaks

If you smell gas, act as quickly as possible, following this procedure:

1 Extinguish all naked flames and turn off heating and cooking appliances.

2 Put out lighted cigarettes.

3 Open up doors and windows and leave them open until the problem has been dealt with and the smell dispersed.

4 DO NOT TURN ON ANY SWITCHES – the spark inside the switch could trigger an explosion.

5 Try to locate the source of the leak – a pilot light that has gone out is the most likely cause.

6 Turn off the gas supply at the mains. This is done by turning the lever which is attached to the inlet pipe to the gas meter.

7 If you can't deal with the problem yourself by, say, relighting a pilot light, call for expert assistance – look under Gas Escapes in the telephone directory.

ROOF LEAKS

There are any number of reasons why a roof could leak – slipped tiles or slates, damaged flashing (sealing) around the chimney or broken ridge tiles. All these are best tackled by an expert because the job is potentially dangerous and requires skill and special equipment. However, there is much that can be done inside the roof space to minimize damage to the rest of the house.

Go up into the loft, taking a torch with you if necessary so that you can see where you are treading. Only tread on joists (beams). If you can lay down walkway boards between the joists, so much the better. Once you have located the source of the problem, lift up any soggy insulation underneath it and lay down old towels to mop up the moisture. Be wary of electric cables and certainly don't tamper with them.

Lay stout planks or boards across the joists directly underneath the hole in the roof and place buckets or bowls on these to catch the drips. Then call for expert help. Until the help arrives, check the bowls and buckets regularly and empty them as necessary.

LEAKING PIPES

Although frost is perhaps the most common culprit to blame for leaking pipes, other causes could be a leaking joint or an accidentally punctured pipe. Ways of dealing with leaking pipes are legion but most boy scout methods don't work and your best bet is to prepare for the event before it happens by keeping an emergency kit handy (see below). Similarly, prevention is better than cure, and this can often be assured by the proper lagging of pipes.

□ **Repairing a burst or punctured pipe**

The procedure is the same regardless of the cause:

1   Locate the exact position of the burst or puncture and mark it with a piece of chalk. Holes in pipes are often tiny and are therefore hard to locate when the water has been turned off, so do this first while the water is still seeping.

2   As quickly as possible after locating the hole, turn the water supply off at the nearest gate valve or at the stopcock on the rising main (see Chapter 1). Drain down the supply by turning on all the taps. It is best to play safe at this stage by switching off the boiler as well.

3   When the supply has been drained, clean up the pipe all around the hole and make sure that it is dry.

4   Mix up some epoxy putty and spread it over the pipe, forcing it well into the hole or crack.

5   Bind waterproof adhesive tape over the repair in a spiral fashion – the tape should extend at least 10 cm (4 in) beyond the hole.

6 Allow the putty to harden – this usually takes 24 hours – before turning the water supply back on.

7 Call a plumber as soon as possible to replace the damaged section of pipe.

☐ Repairing a leaking joint

There are two ways of joining lengths of pipe together – compression joints and capillary joints. A leaking capillary joint is best tackled by a professional in the long term, whereas you may be able to cure a leak in a compression joint permanently by turning the locking nut a quarter turn. In any event, you can stem the water flow:

1 Turn off the water supply to the pipe.

2 Bind waterproof adhesive tape around the joint, following the manufacturer's instructions.

3 If you are in any doubt, call a plumber as soon as possible to rectify the problem permanently.

Emergency plumbing toolkit

To tackle most plumbing problems quickly you will need the following (all items are readily available from DIY superstores and hardware shops):

- Two-part epoxy sealant especially designed for dealing with plumbing repairs
- Waterproof sealing tape, also specially designed for plumbing.

☐ Preventing frozen pipes and cisterns

Pipes freeze up because they are cold. Obvious enough perhaps, but every winter thousands of households suffer the trauma of dealing with frozen pipes simply because the pipes were left unlagged and therefore cold. Be wise and insulate your pipes now.

Most frozen pipes occur in insulated roof spaces or lofts where the temperature can be below zero during cold spells. To keep your pipes warm, wrap them with insulation. The easiest type of pipe insulation to fit comes as flexible foam tubes which slot around the pipes. An alternative is wrap-around glass fibre bandages which are held in place with tape.

You can prevent your cold water cistern from freezing up by lagging with a glass fibre or polystyrene jacket. These are readily available in kit-form from hardware shops.

·4·
GENERAL MAINTENANCE

This chapter shows you how to tackle those aggravating problems that crop up from time to time, such as a dripping tap, a stone-cold radiator, and a plug that needs rewiring. These repair jobs can easily wait for a day or two, but can't be put off forever!

SEALING DRIPPING AND LEAKING TAPS

Taps usually leak in one of two ways – from the spout or from the spindle that surrounds the tap housing. Thankfully, most leaks occur as drips from the spout and these are the simplest to cure. It just means the sealing washer needs replacing (figs. 15 and 16). Before you start any work on the tap, assess which type you have. Pillar taps are the commonest. Supataps are a variation of pillar taps; these are the easiest to deal with because the water supply doesn't have to be turned off before you can start work on them.

☐ Curing a dripping pillar tap

Before you attempt to renew the defective washer, buy a replacement from a hardware shop. To make sure you buy the right washer, simply state the nature of the tap – tap washers come in standard sizes: sink, basin and bath. Then, to replace the washer:

1 Turn off the water supply to the tap (see Chapter 1) and put a plug in the basin, sink or bath so that no small bits and pieces can get lost down the plug hole. Open the tap to allow residue water to drain.

2 Remove the tap handle by loosening the securing screw. This is usually on the top or at the side of the spindle; sometimes it is hidden under a cap which can be levered off.

3 Unscrew the tap cover (shroud), using an adjustable spanner. Blanket the jaws of the wrench with a soft cloth to prevent the tap cover from being damaged.

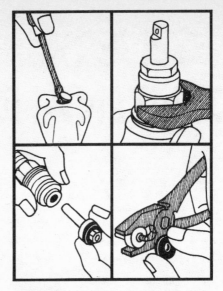

Fig. 15   *Mending a dripping pillar tap.*

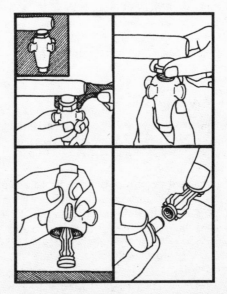

Fig. 16   *Mending a dripping supatap.*

4 With an adjustable spanner, undo the 'headgear' nut (the bottom nut) and lift out the tap mechanism.

5 At the base of the mechanism, you will find a removable 'jumper' or spindle with a washer attached to it. This is the washer that will need replacing.

6 Most spindle washers are held in place with a small nut. Undo this nut with a spanner and lever out the degenerate washer. Fit on a new washer and reassemble the tap.

7 Turn the water supply back on.

□ **Rewashering a supatap**

The great advantage with these taps is that you don't have to turn off the water supply before changing the washer. Another useful feature is that they don't have to be completely dismantled each time. To change a washer:

1 Loosen the retaining nut at the top of the tap with an adjustable spanner.

2 Keeping one hand on the loosened nut, unscrew the tap nozzle. Water will gush out but the flow will stop after you have completely removed the nozzle.

3 Tap the nozzle firmly and the 'jumper' and 'anti-splash' device should fall out.

4 Prise out the combined jumper and washer unit and replace it with a new one.

5 Snap in the new replacement and reassemble the tap.

□ **Curing a leaking tap**

A tap that leaks from the top of the shroud should be tackled by a plumber. The probability is that the washer needs reseating in the base of the tap and this requires special tools.

WIRING A PLUG

This apparently run of the mill chore, that everybody is supposed to know about, has caused more power failures in the average household than anything else. Here's the way to do the job properly (fig. 17):

1 Prepare the flex by carefully slitting the sheath lengthways to about 30 mm ($1\frac{1}{2}$ in). Do this with a sharp handyman's knife, making sure that you don't cut the cores inside. Hold the unwanted sheath away from the cores and sever it as neatly as you can.

▶ *General Maintenance*

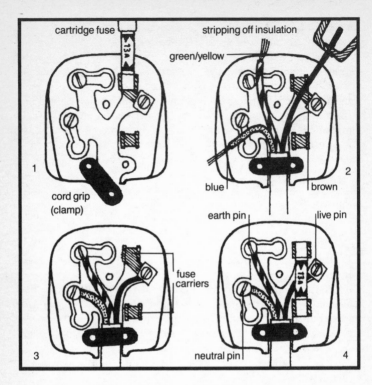

Fig. 17 *Wiring a plug.*

2 Prepare the cores of the flex by stripping off the insulation by 12 mm ($\frac{1}{2}$ in) or so. The best tool for this is a wire stripping tool – this will ensure that you don't cut too many fibres within the flex.

3 Twist the strands of each core together and then thread all three cores underneath the flex clamp in the plug. Each terminal in a plug has a screw-eye or clip into which the cores should be threaded. The *brown* core should go to the *live* terminal (the one that is attached to the fuse); the *blue* core should go to the *neutral* terminal (the one on the left); and the *green/yellow* core should go to the *earth* terminal (the big one at the top).

4 After slotting each core through the terminal slots, screw down the terminal cores. Follow this by clamping the flex securely in the flex clamp. (The outer sheathing of the flex *must* be anchored by this clamp.)

5 Screw or clip the plug cover back into place.

CURING OVERFLOWING CISTERNS

Water cisterns come in two common types: large cold water storage cisterns that are usually found in lofts, and small WC cisterns. The water flow into both types is controlled by a ball valve and this is usually at fault if you notice water gushing from the overflow pipe.

There are two common ball valve designs and they are repaired in slightly different ways. Check to see which type you have by lifting off the top of the cistern. If you notice that the ball has deflated, all you will have to do is get a replacement which you can simply screw on to the end of the arm. However, if the ball is fine, you will have to get a new washer (for a Portsmouth valve), or a new diaphragm (for a diaphragm valve).

□ **Repairing a faulty Portsmouth valve**

To do this you will need a replacement washer, a small screwdriver and a pair of pliers (fig. 18):

1 Turn off the water supply to the cistern. If you are tackling a cold water storage cistern, this will be the stopcock on the rising main (see Chapter 1); if you are dealing with a WC cistern, you should find a gate valve on one of the draw-off pipes at the base of the storage cistern.

2 Unscrew the cap at the end of the valve and remove it. Then, using a pair of pliers, pull out the split pin which secures the float arm. Lever out the float arm.

3 Push the blade of the screwdriver into the slot in the bottom of the float arm and force out the plug from inside the mechanism.

4 Unscrew the end cap on the plug which holds the washer. This is easiest to do using both pliers and screwdriver.

5 Remove the old washer and replace it with a new one.

6 Reassemble the valve and restore the water supply.

□ **Repairing a diaphragm valve**

For this job you will only need a screwdriver and a new diaphragm:

1 Turn off the water supply and unscrew the end cap that supports the float arm. Remove the cap and the attached plunger.

2 Use a screwdriver to ease out the diaphragm inside the valve.

3 Insert the new diaphragm and reassemble the valve before restoring the water supply. Diaphragm valves sometimes accumulate dirt which flows through the water supply. Flush any debris out before inserting the new diaphragm.

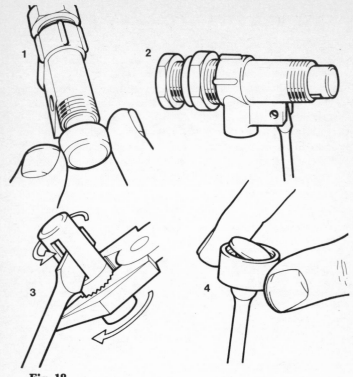

Fig. 18
Mending a ball valve. 1. Take screw cap from the end of the valve. 2. Slide piston out with a screwdriver. 3. Split piston into two parts. 4. Pick out washer with a screwdriver.

DEALING WITH
COLD CENTRAL HEATING RADIATORS

This is quite a common fault and often occurs when the central heating is turned on for the first time after the summer months. The usual cause is an airlock in one or more of the radiators, in which case they will need 'bleeding' – a straightforward task. However, this is not the only cause and if you discover that all the radiators are stone cold or that the radiators furthest from the boiler are cold, your best bet is to call for a heating engineer to have a look at the problem – the radiators may need 'balancing' or there may be a blockage in the pipework.

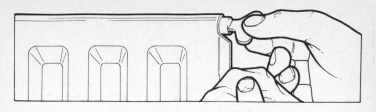

Fig. 19 *Bleeding a radiator.*

□ **Bleeding a radiator**

The only essential tool you need in order to bleed a radiator is a radiator key, which you can get from hardware shops (fig. 19). It's also as well to have a rag and bowl handy to catch drips.

1 Turn the central heating off and locate the bleed valve on the defective radiator. This valve will be at the top at one end of the radiator – it looks like a small square nut inset into a larger hexagonal one.

2 Place a bowl at the foot of the radiator and, using the bleed key, unscrew but don't remove the valve. You should hear a hissing as the trapped air escapes.

3 As soon as water starts to squirt through the valve, tighten it up.

4 Clean up the radiator, and bleed any other cold radiators, before turning the system back on.

DEALING WITH DRY ROT

Dry rot is one of those phrases that turns people pale and sends shivers down their spines. It is caused by a fungus which flourishes in moist (not wet) timber that is relatively warm. The fungus is sinister because it grows rapidly, even through masonry and plasterwork. It is often slow to be detected because it hides behind skirting and floorboards. If you see any cotton-like strands between boards or find any pancake-like fungus growing on timber, you may have dry rot. The spores form a red dust which is a sure sign of its presence. Dry rot is usually accompanied by a rich, musty smell and this is often the first way it is detected.

If you think you have dry rot, act immediately and call an expert to check it out for you. It is seldom worthwhile treating the problem yourself because all the timber around the fungus will have to be cut back and destroyed. Most specialist firms offer a guarantee after treatment and this is well worth having.

▲ *General Maintenance*

·5·

WALLS & CEILINGS

The bottoms of walls tend to get knocked and scuffed easily; decorations get torn or scraped and sooner or later, repairs have to be made. Ceilings escape physical damage but they accumulate dirt and nicotine stains. And then there's always the problem of condensation to deal with, especially in bathrooms and kitchens.

CLEANING WALLS AND CEILINGS

This chore, which is usually done as part of a spring clean or prior to redecorating, can be made much simpler by using the right materials and tools and by rigging up safe and secure 'walkways' from which you can reach the tops of the walls and the ceilings (fig. 20). To construct a walkway, hire a couple of decorators' trestles and some stout scaffolding boards. At first this may seem like an unnecessary expense but it will make the job easier in the long run and it need not cost you much money. If you decide to stick with a stepladder, make sure that it has splayed legs for stability and a safety clip that prevents the legs from spreading apart.

CLEANING WALL COVERINGS AND
PAINTED SURFACES

For this you will need a couple of sponges, a bucket and some sugar soap. Sugar soap is a non-caustic cleaner that gets rid of grease, nicotine stains and general dirt without damaging the surface underneath. It is sold in small or large tubs by most hardware shops.

Before you start, first clear as much furniture as possible from the room and rig up your work platform. Mix up the sugar soap in a plastic bucket, following the manufacturer's instructions. If you are cleaning a wall covering, try the solution on a small inconspicuous corner to see if

Fig. 20 *Using a painting platform.*

the water lifts or damages the paper – not all wall coverings are designed to be washed down, although many are. Then apply the solution to the surface to be cleaned and wipe off the residue with clean water and a fresh sponge. It is best to do the ceilings first and to work systematically across the walls.

CLEANING GLOSS PAINT AND PLASTIC

For this you will need sugar soap, a mild detergent, sponges and a plastic scourer. Clean the paint or plastic as thoroughly as possible with the sugar soap solution (see above). If this doesn't completely do the trick – around a light switch for example – rub mild detergent over the area with a plastic pan scourer. Don't apply too much pressure or you may scratch the surface underneath. Wash the area down after cleaning to get rid of any tide marks.

TOUCHING UP
CHIPPED OR BLISTERED PAINT

The paint on skirting boards and window frames is notorious for getting chipped. It is seldom worth going to the expense and trouble of repainting the whole section of woodwork and a simple touch-up job is usually sufficient. Blistered paintwork is usually caused by moisture in the wood trying to get out and this requires a slightly different treatment.

□ **Chipped paintwork**

To patch chipped paintwork you will need matching gloss paint, a small 12 mm ($\frac{1}{2}$ in) bristle paint brush, white spirit, fine abrasive paper (wet and dry paper) and possibly some cellulose filler and a filling knife as well.

Most chips leave a sharp jagged edge and this must be sanded down smooth so that it is hard to feel when you run a finger over it. If the wood is dented or a chunk has been taken out, mix up some filler and force this into the damaged area with a filling knife. When the filler is dry, smooth it down flush with abrasive paper.

Before painting, clean up the area and brush away any dust or dirt. Then apply the matching gloss, 'feathering' it out towards the edge of the chipped area. Apply two coats of gloss to render the patch invisible. For a really smooth finish, lightly sand down the new paintwork between coats.

□ **Blistered paintwork**

To deal effectively with blistered paintwork, you will need a sharp knife, a small paint brush, some wood primer, as well as matching gloss paint, and some abrasive paper. If you discover a knot in the wood underneath, you will also need some knotting compound which you can get in small bottles.

Cut out the blistered area of paint and allow it to dry for a couple of days. If there is a knot underneath, paint some knotting compound over it to seal it. Then smooth down the edges of the cut area of paint with abrasive paper, clean once again, and apply a coat of wood primer. When this is dry, gently sand it smooth and apply a further two coats of gloss.

PAINTING OVER WALLPAPER

If you don't like the colour or pattern of a wallpaper, it is a simple task to paint over it these days using a 'solid' emulsion. This comes in a sealed paint tray and is applied with a roller. The great advantages of solid emulsions are that they are usually thick enough to cover the wallpaper in one coat, and they don't splash or produce a spray when you roll them out. In other words, you don't have to go through the tedious preparation procedures that are normally associated with painting. All you need for applying solid emulsion is the paint, a roller and a 50 mm (2 in) paint brush.

Move any furniture that could get in the way to the centre of the room, and play safe by spreading a few sheets of newspaper or a dust sheet under the area you are painting. Set up a work platform, if necessary. Clean the wall or walls with sugar soap to get rid of any dirt and then start rolling out the emulsion, starting at the top of a wall and working downwards. Use your brush to apply areas of paint around doors and windows – you will find that the roller can't get into tight angles. When you have completed the wall, wash out the brush and roller in warm water.

WALLPAPER PROBLEMS

Wallpaper is comparatively vulnerable and is therefore subject to wear and tear. For this reason it is worth saving offcuts of paper if you have done any decorating yourself, so you can use these offcuts for repairs in the future.

It is common to find that paper has peeled away from walls at the edges or along the seams – these problems are easily remedied but it is worth finding out exactly why this has happened. It may be because of damp, in which case this should be cured before you go any further (see below).

☐ Patching wallpaper

Assuming you have a suitable offcut with which to make the patch, this is a simple enough task. You will also need wallpaper paste and a stiff brush or sponge:

1 Tear any 'dog ears' from the damaged wallpaper, trying to keep the tears as small as possible. If the wallpaper won't tear, it is probably made of vinyl (see below) which needs to be treated differently.

2 Hold an offcut over the hole and move it around until it matches the pattern exactly.

3 Tear – do not cut – a suitable patch from the offcut. If possible, peel 5 mm ($\frac{1}{4}$ in) of backing paper all around the edge of the patch.

4 Paste the back of the patch with wallpaper adhesive and smooth it into place with a stiff brush or sponge.

☐ Patching vinyl wall coverings

To do this you will need a wallpaper paste that is suitable for using with vinyl wall coverings, sticky tape, a sponge or stiff brush, a sharp knife and a steel ruler:

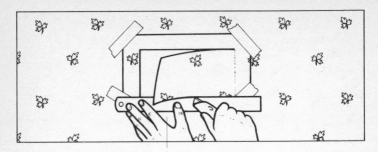

Fig. 21 *Patching vinyl wallpaper.*

1 Hold the offcut over the hole and slide it around until it matches the pattern.

2 Tape the offcut temporarily in place and then, using the ruler and sharp knife, cut a square through both layers of the covering (fig. 21).

3 Remove the old piece of vinyl before sticking the patch in place using the adhesive.

□ **Dealing with lifting seams and corners**

Seams and corners often lift away from a wall because it is damp. If this is the case, check and rectify the cause of the damp before going any further. You will need a filling knife (or an ordinary household knife that doesn't have a sharp point) a sponge, a small paint brush, and some patching adhesive. You can buy small tubes of patching adhesive quite readily from hardware and DIY shops. To apply the adhesive:

1 Slide your knife under the paper to find out how far back you will have to insert more adhesive.

2 Apply adhesive to the back of the paper with the small brush and then smooth the paper down with the sponge.

3 Wipe any excess adhesive off the paper, otherwise this will gather dust and look unsightly.

RENEWING AND CLEANING TILES AND GROUTING

Tiles are tough and durable but they do occasionally crack if they are knocked by something hard. And whereas tiles are relatively easy to keep clean, the grouting between them can become grubby very quickly, especially in damp areas like the kitchen and bathroom.

☐ **Replacing a cracked tile**

This is not always an easy job and you may need some muscle power, especially if the cracked tile has been efficiently stuck down. You will require a hammer, an old chisel, an electric drill and masonry bit, a replacement tile, tile adhesive, a serrated adhesive spreader, and some grout. From the safety angle, it is also a good idea to wear goggles and sturdy gloves.

1   Wearing goggles to protect your eyes from fragments of the tile that may splinter off, drill a hole in the centre of the tile using a large masonry bit.

2   Rake out the grouting all around the tile and then start chipping away with your chisel and hammer. Start chipping in the middle of the tile and work outwards, levering off pieces as you go. Wear gloves when you do this to protect your hands.

3   Scrape away any residue adhesive that remains on the wall with your chisel. Ideally there should be no bumps and lumps remaining.

4   Spread adhesive on the back of the replacement tile with the notched spreader. Don't fall into the trap of applying too much adhesive as this will make a weak fixing.

5   Position the new tile in place and check that it lies flush with its neighbours.

6   After about 24 hours or so when the adhesive should have set hard, regrout around the tile.

☐ **Dealing with grubby grouting**

There are three ways you can deal with dirty or mouldy grouting. The first, but least effective way in the long run, is to wash the grouting down with a proprietary fungicide solution which you can get inexpensively from hardware shops. It is not worth using bleach as this only does a superficial clean-up. Using a fungicide will not cure the problem completely but it will smarten up the grouting for a short time. If you use this, be sure to wear rubber gloves.

The second method is to rake out all the existing grouting with an old chisel or screwdriver and to redo the whole job. This is often the best solution if the area you are dealing with is regularly splashed with water. The best type of grouting to use is a two-part epoxy grout which is both durable and waterproof. Ordinary waterproof grouting is adequate in many damp areas but is not suitable for tiled shower cubicles or work surfaces.

The third method is to touch up the grouting with a proprietary grouting 'paint'.

► *Walls & Ceilings*

□ **Touching-up grouting**

Touch-up paints are easily bought from hardware shops or DIY stores. They are sold in packs which contain most of the tools you need, including an application brush. They come in several different colours so you can change the colour of the grouting if you so choose. The only snag with touch-up paints is that they don't take to waterproof or epoxy grouts.

To apply touch-up paint, first clean off the tiles and grouting with a sugar soap solution and then apply the fluid from the bottle using the supplied brush. After an hour or so, wipe off the excess paint with a damp sponge or cloth and finish off by polishing the tiled surface with a dry cloth.

COPING WITH CONDENSATION AND DAMP STAINS

As we all know, damp can damage decorations and create unpleasant smells. More importantly though, it can also ruin the fabric of a house – the floors and walls – and this can lead to major headaches such as dry rot, damaged wiring and unsafe supporting timbers.

Damp comes in four common forms and it is important to recognize which type you are dealing with before you set about curing it.

Condensation is the most common type of damp inside a house. Its most familiar form is found in kitchens and bathrooms where hot water from taps evaporates and condenses out on cold surfaces like window panes and ceramic tiles. This type of condensation is call *superficial*. Unfortunately another type of condensation occurs, called *interstitial* condensation. Absorbent materials such as bricks and plaster suck up moisture and for a time this can go unnoticed. However, during cold spells, this moisture can condense out inside the bricks or plaster, causing stains and damage to the fabric of the house.

Rising damp is caused by moisture seeping up through the walls of a house. This is usually checked by a damp-proof course (DPC) which is inserted into the outside walls. If, however, you detect mould or damp stains low down on the outside walls of your house, rising damp could be the cause. (See Chapter 7 for advice on how to deal with this problem.)

Penetrating damp arises because of a fault or faults on the outside of a house. If rain or snow is driven against a wall it will seek out nooks and crannies and can penetrate through to the inside of a house, especially if the walls are solid. (See Chapter 7 for advice on how to deal with this.)

Traumatic damp is caused by a burst or leak in the water system.

☐ **Dealing with condensation**

There are many ways of beating condensation, depending on its location and how much money you are prepared to spend.

If the problem occurs in a kitchen or bathroom you can:

● have an extractor fan installed – this is relatively expensive but should solve the problem
● have double glazing installed – with double glazing, the inner pane stays at room temperature so the water vapour won't condense out
● leave a window ajar to let hot, steamy air out
● turn up the central heating – hot air can 'carry' more moisture than cold air so that it won't condense out
● have a tumble drier outlet ducted to the outside – hot air from tumble driers is notorious for creating condensation.

If you notice condensation stains on a chimney breast:

● have a ventilator installed at the base of the chimney breast to allow a draught of air up the chimney (this only applies to chimney breasts that have been blocked up)
● have the flue (casing), that runs up the chimney from a boiler, checked for leaks.

If you have damp ceilings or floors you can:

● fix insulated tiles to the ceiling
● lay a foam-backed foil underlay on the affected floor (check first to see that the problem isn't rising damp); alternatively, you can stick cork tiles to the floor – these are 'warm' and prevent condensation
● cover the affected area with a special anti-condensation paint which will help to prevent moisture forming droplets
● check that there is an adequate draught in the loft (a common area for condensation) by removing insulation material from the eaves. If the problem persists, try laying polythene sheeting under the insulation before contacting a specialist.

If you have damp cupboards:

● place an open jar of silica gel crystals in the cupboard – these absorb

Wall Fixings		Description	Suitable for	Strength
Plastic strip	1	Ribbed plastic strip which is cut to length	Masonry	Good
Fibre plug	2	Pre-cut plugs sold in packets	Masonry	Medium
Anchor plug	3	Plastic arrow head which expands for grip	Hollow walls	Weak
Rubber plug	4	Machine screw with rubber collar	Hollow walls	Medium
Collapsible plug	5	Machine screw with metal 'wings'	Hollow walls	Medium
Gravity toggle	6	Machine screw with metal toggle	Hollow walls	Good
Spring toggle	7	Machine screw with sprung 'wings'	Hollow walls	Good
Nylon toggle	8	Anchor and collar linked with nylon cord	Hollow walls	Good
Petal anchor	9	Plastic plug with expandable 'wings'	Hollow walls and doors	Weak
Plugging compound	10	Powder that is mixed to a paste	Masonry	Good

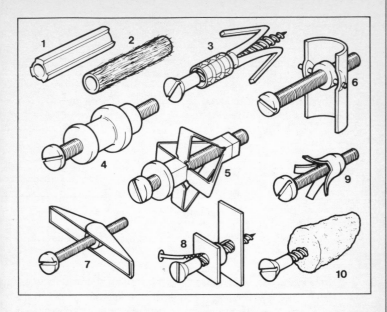

Rawlplug types – see chart opposite.

moisture from the atmosphere, but they do have to be dried out in a hot oven every so often to 'reactivate' them. You can buy silica gel crystals in packs or in specially designed jars

● drill a series of holes in the tops and bottoms of the cupboards. Ideally, the holes should be about 25 mm (1 in) in diameter to allow a draught of air through the enclosed space.

□ **Decorating over damp stains**

Once you have cured the reason for the damp and allowed the moisture to dry out, a damp stain can be safely redecorated. You will need an aluminium primer, finishing gloss or emulsion, a stiff brush and a paint brush:

1 Brush away any mould on the stain.

2 Cover the area with a coat of aluminium primer. If you don't do this, the chances are that the stain will re-emerge in the course of time, even if the damp has dried out.

3 When the primer is dry, brush on a couple of finishing coats of either gloss or emulsion. Alternatively, repaper the wall.

▲ *Walls & Ceilings*

TACKLING LOOSE WALL FIXINGS

Most problems with wall fixings happen because the wrong sort of fixing was used in the first place. These days it is possible to get a fixing that is suitable for just about every type of wall. Before buying a new fixing, check the type of wall you are nailing or screwing into, and also make sure that it is able to carry the weight of what you intend to hang. Your local hardware store may be able to advise you if you are unsure which wall fixing you need (see chart p. 54).

☐ Weak fixings in partition walls

Partition walls are usually hollow and are made from sheets of plasterboard that are nailed up to vertical 'studs'. A fixing into a sheet of plasterboard will not take much weight and, alas, this is where many fixings are sighted. If a picture, shelf, or appliance comes away from a hollow wall, there is only one satisfactory way to deal with the problem:

    1 After lifting away the hanging item, pull out the wall fixing.

    2 Patch up the hole using a standard cellulose filler, smooth the filler down with a fine abrasive paper, and then redecorate to match.

    3 If you suspect that the item was too heavy for a plasterboard-type fixing, search for a stud and add a new screw fixing directly into this. The easiest way to locate a stud is to tap the wall with your knuckles – when you hear a solid thud, you will have found a stud. You will need a drill and suitably sized wood bit (the size is often recommended by the manufacturer of the fixing) and an appropriate screw – a 25 mm (1 in) screw is adequate for most small items. Drill a new fixing hole for the item and twist in the new fixing screw, using a screwdriver.

    4 If the original item is light enough to be supported by a hollow wall fixing, screw this in place, following the manufacturer's instructions carefully.

☐ Weak fixings in solid walls

The simplest way around this problem is to apply the following procedure:

    1 Remove the fixing and tidy up any damage.

    2 Apply an epoxy filler to the hole, forcing it well in, and allow it to dry for 24 hours or so.

    3 Drill a new hole in the filler, using an appropriately sized bit, and screw in the fixing screw.

FLOORS & STAIRS

Floors and stairs receive an inordinate amount of wear and tear, not just from foot traffic but from knocks and spills as well. Keeping them clean and well maintained is essential.

REMOVING STAINS FROM CARPETS

If possible try to treat the stain as soon as it occurs – the longer it is left, the harder it will become to lift. When dealing with a stain, don't fall into the temptation of rubbing it as this will probably force it in deeper. It is far better to try and lift as much liquid from the stain as possible by applying layers of absorbent tissue.

There are many carpet shampoos and cleaners available and they are the best things to use to lift stains. Some are spirit-based and others are water-based and it is important to use a type that is appropriate, or else you may find that the stain won't budge. Drinks, for example, should be treated with a water-based shampoo, whereas greasy stains are best tackled with a solvent-type cleaner.

When using a cleaner, apply it sparingly on a clean cloth – if you pour it on, you will almost certainly drive the stain further into the carpet. Always work inwards from the outside edges of the stain, turning the cloth frequently as it lifts the stain.

For large areas or for really awkward stains, you may have to call in professional help. Alternatively you may be able to hire carpet cleaning equipment from a hire shop. Here are some useful tips for those particularly stubborn stains.

▲ *Floors & Stairs*

Warning about carpet cleaners

Carpet cleaners, particularly spirit-based types, can be dangerous to work with. Play safe when using them by following these tips:

● keep the room well ventilated
● extinguish cigarettes and naked flames
● keep children and pets out of the way
● wear rubber gloves.

Baby stains – sick, urine etc   Scrape away as much as you can with a spoon, then treat with a shampoo. Act quickly as some of these stains can travel through to the underlay which will need more prolonged, and possibly professional treatment.

Blood   Sponge away new blood stains with cold water. Old blood stains are the very devil to remove and professional advice may have to be called in. Murderers, be wary – every blood drop lays a trail!

Chewing gum   Freeze the gum solid by applying chunks of ice wrapped in a plastic bag. This will congeal the gum and make it easier to break up into pieces that can then be lifted from the carpet.

Dyes   How you treat these rather depends on whether it is a cold dye or hot dye. Most DIY dyes are *cold*, which means you should be able to lift untoward spills with copious quantities of cold water. *Hot* dyes, which are set with special chemicals, can only be removed with particular solvents, and these are best applied by a professional.

Fat   This includes oil from cooking and is best treated with a dry-cleaning fluid.

Ink   Treat fountain pen ink with water. If a residue stain is left behind, tackle this with a solvent. Ink from a *biro* should be treated either with a solvent or with methylated spirits.

Milk   This should be blotted with damp rags or cloths as soon as possible, before it has a chance to turn rancid and smell. Treat with shampoo if the stain or smell remains.

Paint   It is important to know which type of paint you are dealing with. Emulsion (water-based) paints can be mopped up with a sponge and a lot of cold water; resin or oil-based paints should be treated with white spirit. However, be warned: white spirit can 'melt' underlay and can tarnish dyes within a carpet. For this reason, it should be applied lightly and if you are in doubt, seek professional advice.

Wax   To clear wax you will need a sheet of ordinary brown paper and an electric iron. Place the paper over the wax and then run the hot iron over the top. The heat will melt the wax which will then be absorbed by the paper.

Wine   Dab the stain dry as soon as possible. It is not always a good idea to apply salt – this may absorb the wine but it can also set the colour fast in the fabric of the carpet. Old stains can usually be dealt with by applying a solvent cleaner or a solution of methylated spirits.

PATCHING CARPETS

In order to patch a small hole or frayed section of carpet you will need a sharp trimming knife, a hammer, some latex carpet adhesive, 30 mm (2 in) wide adhesive carpet tape, a piece of hessian slightly larger than the patch, and an offcut of carpet with which to make the repair (fig. 22).

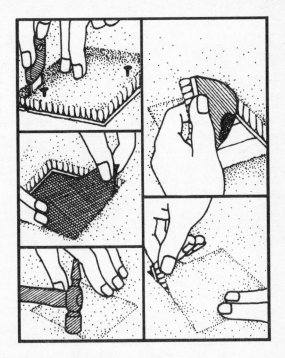

Fig. 22 *Patching a carpet.*

□ Cutting out the patch

1 Lay the new piece over the hole and check that the pile runs in the same direction as the carpet.

2 Hold the offcut firmly in place and then cut through the two layers using a sharp trimming knife. Be sure not to slice through the underlay as well.

3 Lift out the damaged section and try the patch for size.

Your next step will depend on whether the carpet is loose or fitted.

☐ **Patching loose laid carpet**

1 Roll back the carpet and smear latex adhesive around the edge of the hole and the new patch. The latex should go about halfway up the pile.

2 When the adhesive becomes dry to the touch, position the patch in place.

3 On foam-backed carpet, secure the patch in place by laying strips of tape along the edges. With ordinary carpets, cut a piece of hessian about 50 mm (2 in) larger all round than the hole and stick this over the back of the carpet with latex adhesive.

4 Lay the carpet back in place and tap the edges of the join lightly with a hammer. This will help to disguise the join.

☐ **Patching fitted carpet**

1 Push a piece of paper larger than the patch through the hole in the carpet so that it lies on the floor or underlay.

2 Lay a section of hessian, again larger than the hole, so that it is sandwiched between the paper and underside of the carpet.

3 Spread latex adhesive on the hessian and also coat the edges of the hole and the patch.

4 Lay the patch in place and tap the joins lightly with a hammer.

CURING CURLING OR SLIPPING RUGS

A curling corner can often be dealt with by sticking adhesive carpet tape to the underside. If this doesn't work, your best bet is to stick a hessian backing to the rug with latex adhesive.

Slipping rugs are potentially dangerous and the best way of dealing with the problem is to use a non-slip underlay.

DEALING WITH SQUEAKY OR LOOSE FLOORBOARDS

Floorboards tend to start squeaking when the fixing nails become loose or worn. Refixing a floorboard is simple enough. You will need a hammer, a nail punch and some flooring brads. If you don't have any flooring brads, you can use 50 mm (2 in) No 8 screws instead, but this involves more work and is not necessarily more effective.

1 Locate the loose board and then drive in new flooring brads. The brads must sink into the supporting joists, so if you position them next to the existing ones you shouldn't go far wrong.

---

2 Sink the heads of the brads beneath the surface of the timber using a nail punch.

3 Dust the cracks between the boards with talcum powder – this lubricates the edges so that they don't squeak.

4 If the problem persists, you may have to have the floorboard planed down. This is a job for a professional.

FILLING GAPS IN FLOORBOARDS

Gaps in floorboards not only look unsightly if they are exposed but they can also let in draughts, especially on the ground floor, and they can ruin carpets unless there is a thick underlay. There are two ways of filling the gaps, depending on their widths.

☐ Using slivers of wood

This is probably the best method to use if the gaps are wide, say 5 mm ($\frac{1}{4}$ in) or more. You may be able to get slivers of suitable softwood from a timber yard. All you need in addition to the wood is a hammer, saw and abrasive paper:

1 Cut the slivers of wood to length and tap them into the gaps with a hammer.

2 If necessary, sand the strips flush with the floorboards using abrasive paper wrapped around a small block of wood.

☐ Using papier mâché

Papier mâché is an excellent filler. You will need some old newspapers and some wallpaper adhesive, some abrasive paper and possibly some water-based stain:

1 Shred the newspapers and mix them up in a bowl with some thick wallpaper paste. Stir the mush around until it is a consistent pulp.

2 If the floorboards are exposed, add some water-based stain to match the colour.

3 Fill the gaps with the papier mâché and leave it to dry.

4 Sand down the papier mâché until it is flush with the floorboards.

CURING A CREAKING STAIRCASE

Stairs usually start creaking and groaning when the treads or risers are not securely fixed. They often work loose if the atmosphere in the house is hot and dry. There are two ways of tackling the problem – from underneath, which is better, or from above. Sometimes it is not always possible to reach the underside of the staircase but, more often than not, the cupboard under the stairs provides access.

☐ **Tackling stairs from underneath**

To cure a creaking staircase from underneath you may need a wide selection of tools: a G-cramp, drill and bits, screwdriver, bradawl and hammer. You may also need some triangular blocks of wood cut from a piece of 38 mm (1½ in) square softwood, some 75 mm (3 in) No 8 screws and some PVA wood glue (fig 23.).

Stairs are amazingly complex and in most cases the treads and risers are held in grooves with wooden wedges. If you detect that any of these wedges are loose, lever them out, coat them with adhesive, and tap them back into place with a hammer. In many cases this alone may cure the creaks in the staircase.

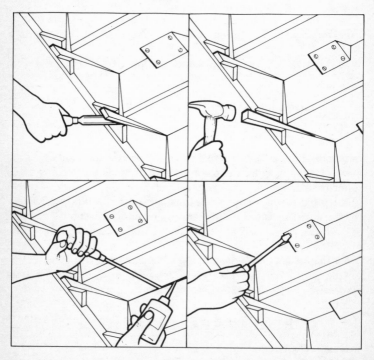

Fig. 23 *Mending a squeaking staircase.*

If the creaks persist, you will have to resort to more drastic measures by fitting supporting wedges into the angles between the defective risers and treads. Two blocks per tread should be sufficient:

1   Cut the triangular sections of wood into 75 mm (3 in) lengths and drill out clearance holes for the screws. Two screws should go into the riser and two into the tread.

2   Hold the blocks in the angle under the tread and make pilot holes in the staircase for the fixing screws, using a bradawl. Try the screws for size and check that they are not long enough to pierce through to the other side of the tread or riser.

3   Coat the edges of the triangular blocks with wood glue and then screw them in place.

4   While you are working on the underside of the staircase, take the opportunity to squirt wood glue into any gaps where the risers and treads meet. If necessary, pin the edges together with 38 mm (1½ in) oval nails.

□ **Tackling stairs from above**

To secure a tread that has separated from the riser below, you will need some 38 mm (1½ in) oval nails, some PVA wood glue, a hammer and a nail punch:

1   Lift away the stair carpet and then lever up the defective tread using an old chisel or screwdriver.

2   Squirt some wood glue into the join and then nail down the tread into the riser, using 38 mm (1½ in) oval nails. Space the nails out at about 30 cm (12 in) intervals or so.

3   Tap the nail heads below the surface of the wood using a nail punch so that they can't cause any damage. If the stairs are to be left uncarpeted, fill over the heads of the nails with a matching wood filler.

ADJUSTING A WORN STAIR CARPET

Stair carpets are subjected to a great deal of uneven wear – the carpet on the edges of the steps tends to suffer more than other areas. The least expensive remedy for this problem is to move the carpet up the stairs by about 10 cm (4 in) or so (fig. 24). This is not a particularly difficult task but it is time consuming and demands care. It is also only worth tackling when there aren't too many people in the house who want to run up and down the stairs.

There are no hard and fast rules for the tools you will need because there are several ways in which a stair carpet can be laid. However,

▶ Floors & Stairs

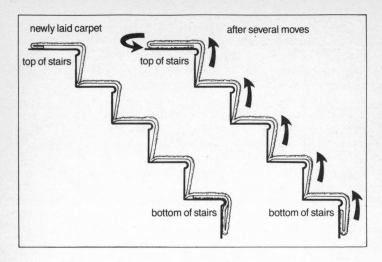

Fig. 24 *Moving a stair carpet.*

you will probably need a tack remover, a small hammer (an upholsterer's hammer is ideal) and a wooden spoon. You may also need a screwdriver. The materials are usualy minimal – some carpet tacks and possibly a strip of underlay:

1   Starting at the top of the staircase, release the carpet from its fixings. This usually means lifting up tacks. It is important to make a mental note of how the carpet is fixed – when it comes to relaying it, you should follow the original fixing method.

2   Roll up the carpet at the top and work down the stairs. If the carpet is fixed with stair rods, slip these out of the way; if it is held in grippers, ease it away from the teeth. Don't pull the carpet sharply away from gripper teeth as this can cause severe damage.

3   Continue down the stairs until you reach the bottom where you will probably find that the carpet has been tucked underneath itself.

4   Copying the original laying method, start refitting the carpet but this time move the carpet up by about 10 cm (4 in) or so. Start at the bottom and work upwards, making sure that the carpet is parallel with the wall.

5   If the carpet is fixed with grippers, force it into the teeth with a wooden spoon; if it is held in place with rods, reinsert these, keeping the carpet taut.

6   When you get to the top, turn the surplus 10 cm (4 in) underneath and tack it to the floor.

EXTERIOR REPAIRS

For obvious reasons, repairs to the outside of a house should be done in dry weather – if you are working high up, it can be positively dangerous to work in damp conditions. Safety is paramount when you are working on a ladder, so take heed.

Safety outside

● If possible, try to avoid using an extension ladder – they are heavy and cumbersome. If you don't have a choice, make sure that the ladder has safety clips that keep it extended.

● When erecting a ladder, position the foot against a wall and push it up above you by walking underneath it.

● The gap between the foot of the ladder and the base of the wall should be about a quarter of the height of the ladder. If the ladder is too steep, it will be dangerous to climb; if it is too shallow it will start bouncing as you go up and this can be dangerous.

● Anchor the bottom of the ladder so that it can't slip. There are several ways of doing this. You can tie it to a stake driven into the earth; you can weight the bottom with a bag of sand; or you can have someone on the bottom holding the ladder steady with a foot propped against the bottom rung.

● If the ground is uneven, position a block of wood underneath one or other of the feet. If the ground is soft, put a board under the feet so that they can't sink into the ground.

● At the top of the ladder, try to tie one of the top rungs to a window frame or screw eye driven into timber. This will prevent the top from slipping. It is also a good idea to tie rags around the tops so that they don't damage any paintwork.

● Never rest the top of a ladder against the guttering – it will almost certainly not be strong enough to take the weight. If you want the ladder to be away from the wall, clip a stand-off frame to the rungs. You can hire these and they are easy to use.

● Never carry heavy weights up a ladder as this can make you lose your balance. You can hire work trays which clip to the frame and allow you to rest paint pots and other items on them.

▲ *Exterior Repairs*

CLEANING GUTTERS

This is one of those chores that ought to be done regularly so that debris and leaves don't pile up. Spring and late autumn are the best times of year. To clean gutters you will need a ladder, a trowel and a hosepipe (or several buckets of water):

1 Before starting on the gutters, plug the tops of the downpipes with rags so that debris can't get into them and cause blockages.

2 Clear as much of the waste from the gutter as you can with a trowel.

3 When all that remains is sandy silt, remove the rags from the downpipes and flush out the gutters with plenty of water, using a hosepipe if available.

CHECKING GUTTERS AND DOWNPIPES

Gutters play a very important role in keeping the outside of your house unsaturated. It is worth keeping an eye on them, especially if they are made of cast iron which rusts and is extremely heavy. In most cases, it is best to get a professional to do major repairs as the job can be difficult and dangerous.

Here are a list of faults to look out for. It's perfectly likely that you will be able to spot weaknesses from the ground:

● Gutters are weakest at the joints. If you see water dripping from a joint, have it repaired. A tell-tale sign that often betrays a faulty joint is a green stain down the wall where algae have taken advantage of the moisture that has dripped down the walls.

● If a gutter sags, the chances are that a bracket has broken off or come loose. This should be replaced as soon as possible to avoid further damage.

● If the gutters don't seem able to take the flow of water while it is raining, it may be because they have fallen out of alignment. Correcting this may mean that some of the guttering has to be dismantled before being replaced.

CLEARING A BLOCKED DOWNPIPE

To do this you will need a large bowl, an old wire coathanger or flexible wire, a broom handle and lots of water:

1 Position the bowl under the bottom of the downpipe. This will catch any rubbish that is flushed down the pipe and prevent it from causing another blockage further down the drain well beyond your reach.

2   Lift as much rubbish as you can from the top of the pipe. Follow this by poking down a wire with a hook bent into the end. Always remember that it is better to try and pull rubbish out rather than push it down. If you push it down, it may consolidate the trouble.

3   When you have lifted out as much debris as you can from the pipe, flush it with water.

4   If the problem persists, try the last resort of ramming down a broom handle.

5   If, after flushing with water, the blockage remains firm, you will have no option but to dismantle the pipe. This can be heavy and tedious work and is best left to a specialist.

6   You may be able to prevent the problem from happening again in the future by covering the top of the pipe with a wire mesh. This will catch leaves which are the usual cause of the problem.

DEALING WITH DAMAGED WOODWORK

Woodwork on the outside of a house takes a fair battering from the elements so it is hardly surprising that it needs touching up and treatment now and again. Some woodwork, the fascia boards for example, may have to be removed before they can be treated or painted. This is work for the experts as dismantling and removing structures high up the walls or on the roof is tricky and dangerous. However, window frames can safely be tackled from a ladder or even from inside the window itself.

☐ Treating rotten timber

If moisture is allowed to creep into timber or if it is sealed in by layers of paint, the wood will eventually start to rot. Treat the problem as it arises and you should be able to save having it replaced. The tools you will need are a shave hook (an old chisel will do), a drill and selection of wood bits, a couple of paint brushes and a filling knife. The materials needed are: liquid wood hardener, wood preservative pellets, epoxy wood filler, fine abrasive paper, wood primer and undercoat and topcoat paints.

While you are working on the wood, it is worth determining why the timber has started to rot. It could be that there is a pocket in the wood which has accumulated water; or there might not be free drainage; it could be that the timber was painted 'too young', while it was still

Exterior Repairs ▶

damp; or it could be that the paint was fractured by a combination of frost and rain. Try to find out the cause, and, if possible, correct it before you start the repair. To treat rotten timber:

1 Using a shave hook or chisel, rake out as much of the rotten timber as possible until you get back to hard, firm timber. If the timber is damp, allow it to dry out – this could take several days so be prepared to protect it from rain by covering it with sheets of polythene which can be held in place with drawing pins.

2 When the raked-out timber is dry, brush on the liquid wood hardener. This is extremely tacky so be careful to avoid getting it on your clothes. Make sure that the hardener is absorbed by all the exposed fibres.

3 When the hardener is dry, drill a series of holes around the damaged section of wood for the preservative pellets, following the manufacturer's recommendations. These pellets dissolve when they become damp, dispersing a substance that seals the timber. They provide protection for the future. After drilling the holes, insert the pellets.

4 Mix up some of the epoxy wood filler following the maker's instructions and fill all the drill holes. At the same time, fill in the damaged area. If the hole is substantial, build up the filler in layers rather than trying to do the job all in one go. Leave the filler slightly proud of the surrounding timber so that it can be sanded down flush.

5 When the filler has hardened, which should happen within a few minutes, sand it down smooth with the wood.

6 Prime the wood, preferably with an aluminium primer, before adding the undercoat and two topcoats. Gently sand down between coats to achieve a high gloss.

REVAMPING EXTERIOR PAINTWORK ON WOOD

There is no more skill required for painting exterior wood than for interior timber. Much of the secret of success lies in the preparation and there is little point in repainting over old, tatty paint. You will require chemical stripping liquid or gel, a stripping knife, fine abrasive paper, paint brushes, rubber gloves, wood primer, undercoat and topcoat. And fine weather!

1 Strip off as much old and blistered paint as you can with the stripping knife. Follow this by brushing on the paint stripper, following the manufacturer's instructions. Wear rubber gloves while you do this.

2   When the stripper has had a chance to work, after 15 minutes or so, set to with the stripping knife, taking care not to gouge out the timber underneath the paint. To get into tight corners, you may need a sharp knife or shave hook.

3   Wash down the wood after you have stripped off the paint and then allow it to dry. When the wood is dry, sand it down gently. The stripper will probably have the tendency to raise the superficial fibres in the wood and this can affect the finished paintwork.

4   Apply the wood primer, followed by the undercoat and topcoats. Sand down between each coat to achieve a high-quality finish.

☐ **Revarnishing exterior woodwork**

This procedure is much the same as repainting exterior woodwork (see above). Make sure that you prepare the timber satisfactorily and check that you apply an exterior grade varnish.

TIDYING SHABBY MASONRY

The walls, rendering and pointing on the outside of a house take a considerable amount of battering so it is hardly surprising that they start to decay in time. Fortunately, much can be done to tatty masonry, provided you tackle the problems as they arise – a severely wrecked wall will need expert attention.

☐ **Cleaning masonry**

To do this effectively, you will need a liquid fungicide (or bleach), a chemical masonry cleaning liquid, an old brush, a wire brush and plenty of water. Before you begin cleaning an exterior wall, check that the reason for the grime, especially if it is green and slimy, is not damp that has penetrated the wall from a leaking gutter or something similar:

1   Remove as much of the superficial dirt as you can with a wire brush. This is a time-consuming chore but is worth it in the long run. Don't be tempted into washing down the wall with a detergent as this can make matters worse. If the stains you are trying to remove are white and powdery, you will have little more to do; this is called efflorescence and is a common, harmless stain.

2   Wearing rubber gloves, wash down the wall with a fungicide or bleach solution (1 part fungicide to 4 parts water). Work the fungicide well into the brickwork with a firm brush.

3 If the stains persist, apply a chemical masonry cleaning liquid, following the manufacturer's instructions. Some of these liquids are acidic, so wear gloves and, if you are working above your head, protective goggles as well.

☐ **Repointing a wall**

If you detect damaged or frail pointing between bricks, you can be sure that the wall needs repointing: the old mortar will have to be raked out and replaced with fresh stuff. This is an arduous business and your best advice is to get someone in to do the job for you.

PREVENTING PENETRATING AND RISING DAMP

There is a subtle difference between penetrating and rising damp. *Penetrating* damp is caused by rain or snow passing through the outside walls or roof of a house; *rising* damp seeps up through the ground. Severe cases of both kinds should be tackled by a firm specializing in damp treatment but sometimes DIY remedies are successful.

☐ **Penetrating damp**

In some cases it is worth hiring a professional builder to cure penetrating damp for you. But you can often cure it yourself by doing one or more of the following, depending on the nature and location of the cause (fig. 25):

● Repoint exterior brickwork or have it done for you. Loose or weak pointing is a common cause of damp in houses with solid walls.
● Check the guttering and downpipes for cracks or weak joints. These problems can often be detected by drip stains down the side of the wall. Old guttering also has a tendency to fall out of alignment, causing rainwater to overflow in heavy storms.
● Have a drip groove inserted in a defective windowsill. All windowsills should have grooves along the underside edges – these guarantee that water doesn't run back underneath and on to the wall.
● Check the state of any exterior rendering. Tap it with a hammer handle – if it sounds hollow, water may be able to get behind it causing severe damp problems inside the house. Rerendering is a job for a professional.

Fig. 25
Common causes of damp.

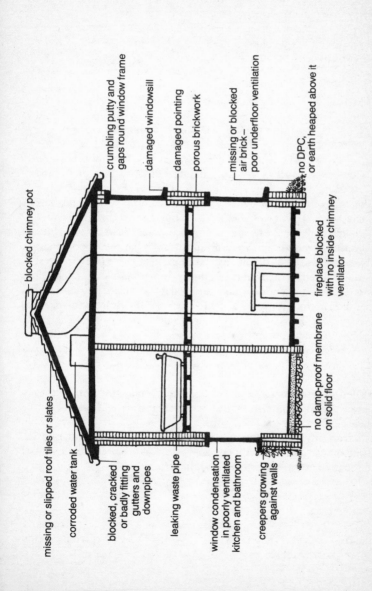

blocked chimney pot

crumbling putty and gaps round window frame

damaged windowsill

damaged pointing

porous brickwork

missing or blocked air brick – poor underfloor ventilation

no DPC, or earth heaped above it

missing or slipped roof tiles or slates

corroded water tank

blocked, cracked or badly fitting gutters and downpipes

leaking waste pipe

window condensation in poorly ventilated kitchen and bathroom

creepers growing against walls

fireplace blocked with no inside chimney ventilator

no damp-proof membrane on solid floor

● Paint the walls with a silicon-based waterproofing liquid. This prevents water from penetrating the brickwork or rendering.
● Check that all perforated airbricks which may surround the base of your house are free from leaves, cobwebs and dirt.
● Have a weather strip and a weather bar fitted to all outside doors so that water can't be blown in underneath them.

□ Rising damp

Rising damp is usually found in walls, although it is also quite common in solid concrete floors. All houses should have damp-proof courses (DPCs) inserted into the walls. DPCs come in many different guises: you may find a black strip of plastic inset in a mortar course about 15 cm (6 in) above the ground; you may find a series of plugged holes in the base of the wall; or you may find a set of 'breathing' tubes. Any of these should be adequate to prevent water from rising up but sometimes the DPC is damaged or bridged. If you don't think your house has a DPC, get it checked by a builder.

Solid floors should be laid over a continuous plastic sheet called a damp-proof membrane. In some houses this is punctured or damaged, rendering it useless. If you have a damp floor, there is a quick test to find out whether the problem is due to rising damp or condensation. Lay a glass tumbler on the floor and bed it in a ring of putty. If, after a couple of hours, droplets of water have formed on the inside of the glass, the problem is rising damp; if the droplets are on the outside, the problem is condensation.

In minor cases, rising damp can be tackled using DIY methods, but if you are in doubt, have the problem checked out professionally:

● DPCs are often covered or bridged by piles of earth, or even flowerbeds, that butt up against the side of the house. Clear away any such piles, so that the DPC is free.
● Penetrating damp can be sealed out using a moisture-curing urethane varnish or a rubber-based paint. When using these, follow the manufacturer's instructions to the letter.

·8·

FURNITURE REPAIRS

Some furniture repairs need special tools such as upholstery needles and cramps. Craft shops are probably the best place to get these – you should be able to find them in the *Yellow Pages*.

STICKING DRAWERS

If you have one drawer that sticks in a chest of drawers containing two or more drawers of similar size, try swapping them around – this sometimes does the trick. Another tip that often works is to remove the drawer and to rub candle wax along the runners. This acts as a lubricant, but don't be tempted to use oil as this will swell the wood and eventually turn sticky, making the problem worse. If the problem persists, you will have to smooth down the runners with abrasive paper. For this you will also need a stick of chalk:

1 Remove the drawer and run chalk along the runner guides.

2 Push the drawer back in and then remove it once more – the chalk will rub away where the runners are sticking.

3 Gently sand down the wood where it is catching and replace the drawer.

DAMAGED FURNITURE

Wooden furniture is easily damaged in a number of different ways – it can be stained, scorched, dented and scratched. Each problem requires a special technique to put it right.

☐ Stains

Before tackling marks, try to determine what caused the problem in the first place and whether it is just the polish which has been stained or the wood underneath.

Alcohol stains are usually superficial and to get rid of them you will need turpentine, linseed oil, wax polish (or an appropriate finish) and plenty of clean rags:

1 Using a clean cloth, rub over the stain with a mixture of turpentine and linseed oil until the marks disappear.

2 Rub on some more polish until the sheen returns to the piece of furniture.

Heat rings, which are left behind by such things as cups of coffee, are caused by a combination of heat and water. You can try a proprietary heat mark remover but if this doesn't work, you will have to remove and then replace the polish on and around the stain. Turpentine (not white spirit), linseed oil, and cloths are what you need, as well as some cigarette ash!

1 Mix up some cigarette ash with a drop of water and rub this over the heat marks – the ash acts as a mild abrasive. Follow this with a mixture of turpentine and linseed oil.

2 When the stains have been lifted, repolish the table.

☐ Scratches

Provided they are not too deep and require filling, scratches can usually be disguised by rubbing on a proprietary scratch polish. You can get scratch polish from most good hardware shops. If the scratches are deep, rub a stick of beeswax over them – this essentially fills them up. Finish off by applying ordinary furniture polish.

☐ Dents

Dents can often be lifted by steaming. For this you will need an electric iron and a clean damp rag:

1 Place the rag over the dent and heat it with the tip of the hot iron. When the rag starts to steam, remove the iron.

2 Repeat the process every half hour or so until the wood swells up, causing the dent to disappear.

3 Polish the furniture to complete the repair.

☐ Burns and scorch marks

These can be removed, provided they are small, but a slight depression will be left in the wood. You will need some turpentine, linseed oil and some flour paper (very fine abrasive paper):

1   Remove the polish or varnish by rubbing on turpentine and linseed oil.

2   Smooth away the scorch mark by rubbing over it with flour paper. It is better to leave a shallow depression rather than a dent.

3   Repolish when the marks have been removed.

WEAK JOINTS

Joints tend to work loose when furniture is abused in some way – chairs are particularly vulnerable because they are rocked back on and used as 'hop-ups'. However, central heating is also a common cause – all wood contains moisture and when this starts to dry out, the wood shrinks, causing the joints to spring apart. Never keep good pieces of furniture near radiators or fires. It is not a good idea to try and repair valuable or delicate furniture especially if it has complicated joints – you would be advised to hand it over to a professional furniture repairer.

Furniture can be jointed in many different ways but repairs usually follow a similar procedure – you have to dismantle the joint and then reassemble it using fresh glue. You will need a hammer, several rags, PVA wood adhesive, a sharp chisel or trimming knife, a pair of pliers and a cramp of some kind – tourniquet cramps are most frequently used in furniture restoration:

1   If the joint is fixed with screws or nails, remove these as the first step to dismantling the joint.

2   Wrap some rags around the head of your hammer and gently tap the joint apart. You shouldn't have to use a great deal of force – several taps are better than one heavy blow.

3   When you have separated the joint, clean out any old glue that remains. This will probably be hard and brittle and can be scraped off with a sharp chisel or knife.

4   Smear fresh PVA adhesive on the mating parts of the joint and reassemble the furniture.

5   Wipe away any excess adhesive that oozes out and then cramp the joint tightly together. Protect the furniture where the cramp touches it with rags or small blocks of wood so that it does not get damaged.

HANDLES

Handles that have worked loose can be extremely aggravating but thankfully they are usually easy to put right. The bolt-on variety can usually be tightened up at the back, using an adjustable spanner. If

▶ *Furniture Repairs*

necessary, fit an extra washer. Handles that are dowelled or screwed on require a bit more effort but you only need some PVA wood adhesive, some matchsticks and possibly a screwdriver.

1 Remove the handle and scrape away any old glue that remains.

2 Pack out the fixing hole or holes with a matchstick or two smeared with adhesive.

3 Refit the handle and it should be as good as new.

HINGES

Squeaky hinges usually just need a drop of light oil on them. Don't overdo the oil or else it will drip down the sides of the doors. If a door keeps springing open, it may be because the hinges have been set too deep into their recesses. You can cure this problem by packing out the recesses with strips of card. You will need a screwdriver, some card and a pair of scissors:

1 Unscrew the hinges from the frame. Tackle the bottom ones first or else the door may strain the fixings.

2 Cut strips of card to the same size as the hinge recesses and pack them in place.

3 Screw the hinges back to the frame, the top one first.

CUPBOARD DOORS

If a cupboard door starts to stick, try to find out the reason. If may be that it has dropped on its hinges or it could be because it has swollen due to moisture being absorbed – many people find that their doors stick more in the spring after the central heating has been turned off.

If the hinge screws have started to pull out, remove the door (see above) and fill the screw holes with glued matchsticks. If, after replacing the doors, the hinges are still weak, have them replaced or fit bigger screws.

If the door is snagging on the frame, you will have to sand down the area with abrasive paper. You will obviously need a screwdriver to remove the door and you may need paint and painting equipment:

1 Unscrew the hinges, starting at the bottom, and lift off the door. It may be heavier than you think, so get help if necessary.

2 Wrap a sheet of abrasive paper around a block of wood and sand down the edge where it catches. You probably won't have to remove very much timber.

3 Try out the door again by fixing it back in the frame.

4 It is best to paint over the area that you have sanded so that the wood is sealed. Apply a wood primer first and then a couple of layers of topcoat.

□ Kitchen cupboard doors

Modern kitchen unit doors are usually hung on concealed hinges which enable you to adjust the alignment. If a kitchen cupboard door catches, try adjusting one of the screws (fig. 26).

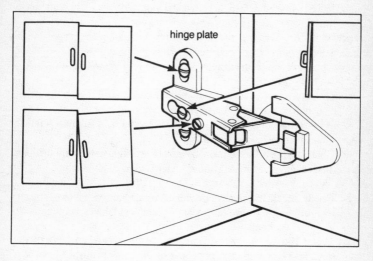

hinge plate

Fig. 26   *The concealed hinges on a hinge plate.*

VENEER

Veneer that has blistered or buckled is not easy to stick back down again – your best bet would be to take the piece to a professional restorer who will probably treat it with steam. However, if a flat sheet of veneer has started to lift, it is straightforward to stick back down again. PVA adhesive, and a scraper of some kind are all you require to do the job:

1   Lift up the veneer and scrape away any old glue that remains.

2   Spread a fine film of adhesive on the base wood and smooth the veneer back down. Don't apply too much adhesive as it is water-based and may cause the wood to swell and buckle.

3   Place some heavy books on top of the veneer until the adhesive has had a chance to dry.

Furniture Repairs

WOODWORM

Woodworm is not as serious as rot but, given time, it can seriously weaken and disfigure wooden furniture and timbers. The most obvious signs of woodworm are the tiny holes which are made by grubs boring their way through the timber. Not all woodworm holes are 'active' – there may not be any grubs inside the wood. The only true sign of active woodworm is a fine dust, called frass, which is left behind by the grubs. Frass is often found underneath infected furniture and structural timbers. If you notice frass, or suspect that you have active woodworm in structural timbers like joists and floorboards, have it treated by a pest control company who will spray all exposed wood with insecticide. However, there is no reason why you shouldn't treat woodworm in furniture yourself.

To do this you will need a woodworm treatment fluid which is either sold in cans or aerosols. In addition you will need a filler paste (brummer paste) or a stick of beeswax, and some furniture polish which is resistant to woodworm.

1 Clean up the affected piece of furniture and take out any drawers or shelves – each component should be treated even if you can't see any holes.

2 Brush or spray the woodworm treatment over the timber, following the manufacturer's instructions. Wear gloves while you do this as some treatments are toxic.

3 Using the fine nozzle supplied with the treatment, squirt the liquid into all the woodworm holes. This is time-consuming but it is worth doing thoroughly.

4 Leave the treatment for a day or so to take effect, then wipe off any excess liquid. Don't stand the furniture on a carpet as the liquid can cause stains.

5 Fill the woodworm holes with brummer paste – you can smear this on with a finger. Alternatively, rub over each hole with a stick of beeswax to fill them in.

6 Finally, polish the piece of furniture with a woodworm-resistant wax polish. An option to this is of course to paint the item.

DAMAGED ENAMEL

Chipped or scratched enamel will inevitably lead to the exposed metal rusting. Baths and cookers are often enamelled, so keep an eye out for chips and tackle them as soon as possible. You will need wet and dry paper, some matching enamel paint and a brush:

1 Rub down the chipped area with wet and dry paper. Add water while you do this to lubricate the abrasive. Sanding down in this way will smooth the edges of the chip and will lift rust on the metal as well.

2 Wipe down the area with a clean rag and then brush on some enamel paint. Enamel paint isn't in fact enamel but it is hardwearing and will protect the metal.

3 When the paint is dry – after 12 hours or so – rub it down gently with wet and dry paper and then apply a second coat.

HARD WATER STAINS

Hard water stains on baths and basins are caused by calcium which is deposited on the surface. Stains like these can often be eradicated by rubbing a fresh lemon over them – the acid in the lemon counteracts the alkali in the calcium. You can also use special proprietary products to remove hard water stains but be warned: some of these may damage the surface of the bath or basin.

UPHOLSTERY

Tears, holes and rips in upholstery are usually quite simple to repair or patch but you may need some special tools and equipment which you should be able to get in large department stores.

☐ Seam tears

To repair a ripped seam you will require a curved upholstery needle, some large pins and some strong thread:

1 Fold under the torn edge that is opposite the seam.

2 Pull or push the folded edge up and over the seam and hold it in place with large pins.

3 Using a curved upholstery needle and strong thread, stitch the fold to the seam. Use a slipstitch so that the repair is almost invisible (fig. 27).

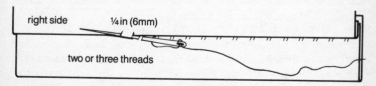

Fig. 27 *Slipstitch.*

▶ *Furniture Repairs*

□ Open tears

Tears that are not near a seam should be patched rather than sewn. If possible cut a patch from matching fabric, otherwise use a fabric of similar weight. Scissors are the other things you will need:

1   Cut away any frayed strands from the edge of the tear. Try not to snip the fabric itself as this will make matters worse.

2   Cut a patch slightly larger than the tear, and slip this underneath, matching the pattern if possible.

3   Lift up the edges of the rip and spread some adhesive on the underside of each one.

4   Squeeze the edges of the tear together, pushing them down on to the patch. Hold the edges like this until the adhesive sets.

□ Holes

Holes can be tricky to repair and you certainly need a steady hand. Sharp scissors and latex adhesive are essential and you may find that some small tweezers come in handy:

1   Cut out a patch for the hole. This should be slightly bigger all round and the weave and pattern should match the main fabric.

2   Spread a film of latex adhesive around the edge of the patch. Try not to get any adhesive in the centre as this will show up when the patch is in place.

3   Slide the patch under the hole. Try not to let the edges turn over – a pair of tweezers is the best tool for holding them flat.

4   With the patch in place, turn over the edges of the hole on to the adhesive underneath.

5   Press the edges flat and weight the repair down until the adhesive dries.

□ Replacing buttons

You really need a double pointed upholsterer's needle to sew buttons on to upholstery properly. The needle should be about 15 cm (6 in) long. When you buy your needle, buy some button twine at the same time (fig. 28):

1   Thread the needle – but don't knot the twine – and push the unthreaded end into the button's position on the fabric. Keep pushing until the unthreaded end appears at the back of the furniture and the eye disappears into the padding.

2   Push the needle back again so that the point emerges just to the side of the original entry point.

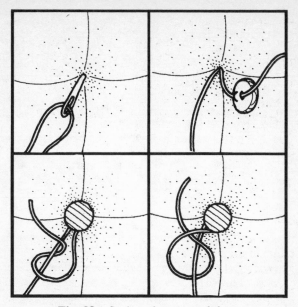

Fig. 28   *Sewing a button on upholstery.*

3   Pull out the needle and pull through the twine so that you have two strands of equal length.

4   Thread on the button and tie a slip knot.

5   Slide the knot up until the button is held firmly in position. Then tie a half-hitch knot and pull the thread tight.

6   Tie the ends of the twine together and snip off the unwanted lengths.

VINYL

Vinyl can be repaired rather like fabrics except that adhesive is used instead of needle and thread. Vinyl adhesives 'weld' surfaces together – there are several different makes but they all work on the same principle.

☐ Tears

Sticky tape, vinyl adhesive and possibly a patch are what you need:

1   Large tears need a reinforcing strip of vinyl to lie underneath them. Cut a strip slightly larger than the tear itself. Reinforcing strips are not necessary for small rips.

2   Coat the strip with a thin film of adhesive and slide it under the tear. Bring the two edges of the rip together and press them down on the strip. If the tear is a long one, hold the edges together with short bits of sticky tape laid across the join.

3   Apply a thin bead of adhesive along both edges of the tear – the adhesive will join them together.

4   After half an hour or so the adhesive should have done its job. If necessary squeeze on a second bead of the glue.

5   If the adhesive is shiny, rub it down to a matt finish with a wad of wire wool.

☐ **Holes**

The important thing to remember when patching a hole is that the edges must not overlap:

1   Cut out a rectangular patch, slightly larger than the hole with a pair of scissors or a sharp knife.

2   Lay the patch over the hole and cut around it into the vinyl underneath – this way you will get a perfect fit.

3   Remove the damaged piece and slot in the patch.

4   Lay a bead of adhesive along the touching edges.

5   If the patch is going to take a lot of strain, you can always reinforce it by gluing strips of matching vinyl underneath the edges.

REPAIRING BROKEN GLASS, CHINA & PLASTICS

One of the most difficult parts of gluing broken objects is holding the bits together while the glue sets. There are a number of tips which can make this easier. However, the first step is to choose the right adhesive. Epoxy adhesives give the strongest bond and are the only realistic choice if an object is going to be regularly washed up in hot water. Whichever type of adhesive you choose, it's always a good idea to have some suitable cleaner or solvent nearby so that you can clean up any spills. This is particularly important when using superglues. It is also not a bad idea to wear rubber gloves, especially if you have sensitive skin – some glues and cleaners can bring out rashes.

When mending plastics, the right glue is sometimes essential – not all plastic glues mend all plastics!

PREPARING CHINA FOR MENDING

It is essential that the broken pieces are clean and dry before you go about gluing them together. And it is also worth remembering that if you are repairing white china, a little titanium dioxide powder mixed into epoxy adhesive will give a good match. You can buy 'titanium white' from good artists' suppliers. You may even be able to mix other powder colours into adhesive to achieve other hues – it's always worth experimenting:

1   Clean up the bits of china using methylated spirits or nail varnish

remover. All the surfaces must be free from grease, oil and any residues of old adhesive. Scrub really grubby edges with an old toothbrush.

2 Clean and dry all the pieces. If they are small, it is a good idea to leave them in a warm oven for 20 minutes.

3 If there are lots of pieces, work out how they all fit together. You will almost certainly find it easier if you stick the bits together in stages.

4 Decide on how you are going to support the pieces while the glue dries (see below).

PREPARING GLASS FOR MENDING

For the best joins, and even these won't be completely invisible, use a special glass adhesive. With these adhesives, surfaces have to be prepared by rubbing them with wet and dry abrasive paper – this provides a key for the adhesive.

You can support ornaments and glasses using one of the methods described below, but some glass adhesives are set by daylight so this should not be obscured. If you are in any doubt, refer to the manufacturer's instructions.

SUPPORTING CHINA AND GLASS

Detailed below are just a few ways of holding pieces together while the glue sets (fig. 29).

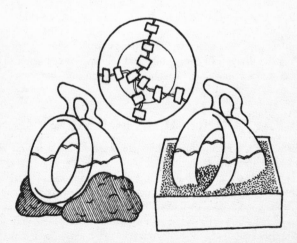

Fig. 29 *Supporting broken china during repair.*

☐ **A sand box**

This is ideal for supporting cups and mugs while their handles are
glued back in place:

1 Fill a bowl or box with silver sand which you can get from most
builders' merchants.

2 Push the item into the sand so that the handle will stand up
vertically.

3 Apply the adhesive to the broken surfaces and wipe off any excess.

4 Leave the item for the appropriate time. It is worth checking the
repair every so often to make sure that the join is perfect – sometimes
pieces slip. The surest way of telling that the join is accurate is to run a
finger over it.

☐ **Putty or plasticine**

Either putty or plasticine will hold pieces together while adhesive sets.
If you are using a special glass adhesive, don't obscure the light from
the join – just support the pieces on the putty or plasticine.

☐ **Sticky tape**

Tape is fine for holding pieces together provided that there is no excess
adhesive oozing out of the join and on to the tape. Always lay tape
across a long join, never along it.

☐ **Elastic bands**

Provided they are not too tight, elastic bands are ideal for holding
broken cups and glasses together. Again, make sure that no adhesive
gets on to the rubber.

☐ **An open drawer**

The bottom half of a plate that has broken cleanly in two can be held
vertically in an open drawer. Rest the other half on top while the glue
sets.

MENDING RIGID PLASTICS

It is never easy to tell one type of plastic from another – if you're not
sure of the type, play safe and use an epoxy resin adhesive for a strong
bond or a superglue if looks are more important.

▶ *Broken Glass, China & Plastics*

☐ **Chips and breaks**

Cleaning up the edges to be joined is especially important with plastics – you will need rags, wire wool and methylated spirits for this:

1 Scrub away any dirt on the faces to be joined with wire wool. This will also key the faces ready for the adhesive.

2 Wipe over the edges with a rag dipped in methylated spirits. This will get rid of oil and greasy marks which could stop the adhesive from sticking.

3 Apply the adhesive, following the manufacturer's instructions. Press the edges together and support the pieces using one of the methods described above.

☐ **Holes**

Small holes and cracks can be filled using an epoxy paste – a strong filler which is mixed with a hardener. Abrasive paper, a filling knife and possibly paint are what you need. If the hole is large, you can get some special wire mesh which will reinforce the repair:

1 Clean the edges of the hole, making sure that all the grease and dirt is completely removed.

2 Dry the edges and then roughen them with abrasive paper to provide a key for the filler.

3 Mix up the adhesive, following the manufacturer's instructions. In most cases you will be required to squeeze out equal lengths of the filler and its hardener and then mix the two together.

4 Try to use the filler quickly – as soon as the hardener is mixed in, it starts to go off and becomes increasingly hard to work. Spread the filler into the hole, using a filling knife. Leave the filler slightly proud of the edges of the plastic so that it can be sanded down smooth when it has hardened.

5 Leave the filler to harden for 15 minutes or so, then sand it down with abrasive paper.

6 Touch up the repair with paint if looks are important.

·10·

DOORS & WINDOWS

Doors and windows suffer a lot of strain, so it is hardly any wonder that they occasionally need touching up or repairing. Some repairs are straightforward, others require a little skill and special tools.

STICKING DOORS

The two most common reasons for a door binding in its frame is either because it has expanded by absorbing moisture from the atmosphere or because it has slipped on its hinges.

☐ Expansion problems

There are a range of remedies from the simple to the difficult. Try out the basic cures first and see if they have any effect. If not, you will have to resort to taking the door off its hinges – something you may prefer to leave to a builder. The equipment you may need ranges from a candle and a screwdriver to a planer file and painting tools:

1 Rub a candle along the opening edge of the door. This is sometimes enough to lubricate the action.

2 If this doesn't work, take a look at the hinges. If any of the screws are loose, tighten them up. If the screws don't appear to bite into the wood, you will have to remove them, the hinges and the door to solve the problem: plug the old holes with dowels and refit the screws (see below).

3 If you still have no luck, try to determine where the door is binding in the frame. This isn't always as easy as it sounds and it is helpful to have a sheet of carbon paper: close the door on to the carbon paper – where it rubs will be a high spot and where the problem lies.

4 Having marked the high spot, start taking the door off the hinges. You will almost certainly need help to do this and it is a good

▲ *Doors & Windows*

· 87 ·

idea to knock a couple of wedges under the door to take its weight while you undo the screws. Start at the bottom and work upwards. If a screw is obstinate, tap it with a hammer – this often loosens the threads.

5 With the door off its hinges, plane down the edge that you marked as a high spot. If you don't have a plane, a planer file is adequate. Work inwards from the edges and don't take off more than a couple of millimetres or you will end up with a draughty door.

6 Hang the door back in its frame, fixing the top hinge first.

7 If the problem has been cured, seal up the sanded edge with a coat of primer and two topcoats so that moisture won't be able to get into the wood and cause the problem again.

8 You may find that during the dry summer months, the door lets in draughts. If this is the case, fit a draught excluder (see below).

☐ **Hinge problems**

One way of checking to see if the door has slipped on its hinges is to hold a spirit level up against the opening edge. If the edge is not vertical the chances are that the top hinges have sprung loose. This is often caused because the hinge recesses are too deep. A sheet of card, dowels and a hammer and screwdriver are what you need:

1 Unscrew the hinges and lift away the door (see above).

2 Tap short lengths of dowel into the old screw holes and then cut out pieces of card to the dimensions of the recesses. Pin or glue the cards into the recesses.

3 Rehang the door and all should be well.

STICKING WINDOWS

There are two types of window: casement and sash (fig. 30). Each type has its own particular problems. Some of the reasons for sticking windows are the same as those for doors – swollen timber and slipped hinges. However, before resorting to any of those solutions, try out this remedy:

1 Open up the window and clear out any dirt, grime and debris that may have collected in the frame. Remove oily patches with a rag dipped in methylated spirits.

2 Locate the area where the window is jamming and try rubbing it down with abrasive paper – it may be that when the window was decorated, paint ran to the bottom causing a build up and a sticking problem. Rub gently so that you don't remove all the layers of paint.

3 If the window still doesn't close and open freely, use a planer file

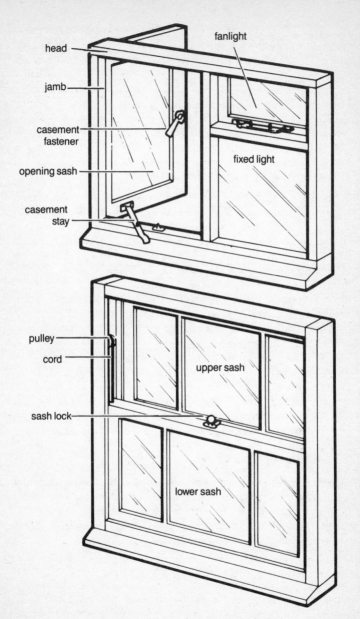

Fig. 30 *Casement and sash windows.*

▲ *Doors & Windows*

to smooth down the wood. Again, don't remove too much or you will end up with draughts whistling through. If you plane through to the wood underneath, seal it with paint, or else the problem will only recur.

SASH WINDOWS

Sash windows are attractive and practical but the older they get, the more prone to problems they tend to become.

□ Rattling and jamming sashes

The beading which holds the sashes in place is the usual cause of rattling and jamming – either the beads are too far apart or they are too tight. However, before touching the beads, check that the cords are running freely over the pulleys at the top – sometimes these can get stuck or the cord slips off. To remove and refix the beads isn't particularly difficult – an old chisel, a pin, a pin hammer and some 38 mm (1½ in) panel pins are what you need:

1 Lever off the beads using an old chisel or screwdriver. Take care not to bruise the wood by levering the chisel on an offcut of wood. If the beads are solidly imbedded in paint, cut through the layers with a sharp knife before you start levering.

2 Tidy up the beads and remove ragged bits of paint, then reposition them in the frame – closer to the sash if you want to stop rattling, further away if you want to let the sash run more freely.

3 Fix the beading in place with panel pins driven in every 30 cm (12 in) or so. Tap gently so that you don't split the timber.

4 Try the window and, if necessary, repaint the beads.

□ Broken sash cords

In theory, repairing a broken sash cord appears simple but it is seldom that. The weights slide up and down in compartments on either side of the window and in order to replace a broken cord, you have to gain access to the weights – doing this can be difficult. For this reason, get in a builder or handyman to do the job for you.

CURING DRAUGHTS

Manufacturers bring out new gadgets and materials for sealing windows and doors every year. Some are better than others and prices can vary too. As a rule of thumb, it is best to avoid the cheapest types because they tend not to last very long. Some draughtproofing strips can be used on either doors or windows but some are specific, so check before you buy.

☐ Self-adhesive foam strips

These are the cheapest of all, and they tend not to last for very long, but they are easy to fit in either window or door frames. One word of warning: foam strips should not be painted over as this will render them useless:

1 Clean up the rebate of the frame so that there are no traces of dust (adhesive won't stick properly on dirt).

2 Unroll the strip, sticky side down, on to the inside of the rebate so that it will be squeezed when the window or door is shut. Cut pieces to length with a pair of kitchen scissors.

3 Foam strips should be replaced every year. To remove traces of old adhesive after you have pulled away the foam, use a rag dipped in white spirit.

☐ Wiper seals

These are specifically designed for use with sash windows. They are made from either plastic or bronze and come in kits containing everything you need apart from a hammer and a pair of scissors:

1 Cut the strip into suitable lengths with a pair of kitchen scissors.

2 Pin the strips against the gaps, using the nails provided. Space the nails about 15 cm (6 in) apart.

☐ Mastic sealant

This is invaluable if you have draughts coming in behind the *frame* of a door or window. It is normally sold in cartridges for use with a special applicator gun – you can buy both in DIY superstores:

1 Clean up the woodwork and masonry on either side of the gap that is letting in the draught. A stiff brush is usually adequate. Sealant can only be applied to surfaces that are completely dry, so if necessary wait until fine weather.

2 Snip off the end of the tapered nozzle to match the width of the gap.

3 Squeezing the trigger on the applicator gun as you go, run a bead of mastic into the gap.

4 To finish off the bead and to make it smooth, run a wet finger along it.

▲ *Doors & Windows*

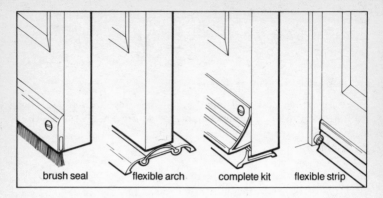

Fig. 31 *Common types of floor seal, attached to the door.*

☐ Pin-on seals

These are usually designed for fitting into door frames although you may be able to use them on casement windows as well. Traditional types of pin-on seals are made from bronze or brass but modern types use plastic. Scissors and tack hammer are the tools you need:

1 Clean up the rebates, then cut the seals to length with a pair of scissors or a hacksaw.

2 Use the pins supplied with the strip to fix the seal, making sure you get the seal the right way round.

☐ Floor seals

There are literally hundreds of floor seals which all attempt to do the same job (fig. 31). Some come in two parts (one is fixed to the floor, the other to the door) and some are just fixed to the door. For most internal doors, a type which is just screwed to the base of the door is sufficient. Brush types are good for carpeted floors because they don't present a trip hazard but on external doors, a two part type with an integral weather bar is best.

Fixing methods vary and there are no hard and fast rules – it is best to follow the manufacturer's instructions.

☐ Letter flap seals

Letter flaps can let in howling gales and this problem can be cured by fitting a brush letter flap seal. These are just screwed over the opening.

EMERGENCIES & FIRST AID

In an emergency dial 999 and ask for an ambulance. If you suspect that you or your casualty has suffered an injury that you can't cope with, don't hesitate (thousands of injuries are made worse by well-meaning people who don't genuinely know what they're doing). When you dial you will be asked four main questions, so have your answers ready. You will be asked:

● whether you want police, fire brigade or ambulance
● the address and telephone number of the place where the injured person lies
● your name and telephone number
● the nature of the injury (bleeding, unconscious, internal etc).

FIRST AID

☐ Breathing

If you find someone who doesn't appear to be breathing, follow these steps:

1 Lay the person on his back and open up the airway by tilting his head back.

2 Push the lower jaw forward so that the tongue doesn't block the passage.

3 Remove any foreign matter from the mouth.

4 Pinch the casualty's nostrils with one hand and hold the jaw with the other.

5 Gently blow into the mouth.

6 Repeat until the casualty starts breathing.

☐ Bleeding

1 Raise the bleeding area so that it is above the heart.

▶ *First Aid*

2   Apply pressure to the bleeding area to stem the blood flow.

3   Bind a sterile bandage around the wound.

4   Call for help if the blood continues to flow and look for signs of shock (see below).

☐ Back injury

1   If you are the casualty, don't try to move if you feel extreme pain – you only have *one* spinal cord. Call for help.

2   If you find someone with a suspected back injury, tell him not to move (movement can cause pain and can also aggravate a back injury). Try to make the casualty as comfortable as possible: place cushions or anything soft along his sides. Don't lift or support the head (the neck is a likely area for a fall injury) but do talk to the injured person to keep morale high.

3   Call for an ambulance.

☐ Broken bones

1   Don't try to move the casualty unless he is in danger.

2   Keep the casualty warm and as comfortable as possible.

3   Support the injured part with your hands or with padding.

4   Call for an ambulance.

☐ Burns

1   Remove the casualty from danger and douse the fire.

2   Hold the burnt area under cold running water for at least 10 minutes.

3   Cut away any clothing from around the burn but don't try to remove anything that is sticking to the burn.

4   Protect the injury with a sterile dressing. Do not put any oily substance, cotton wool or an adhesive dressing on the burn.

5   Call for an ambulance or doctor.

☐ Electric shock

1   Break the current by switching off at the mains.

2   Look for signs of burns and check that the casualty is breathing.

3   Lay the person on his side.

4   Call an ambulance.

☐ Shock

Signs of shock are:

● skin goes very pale and grey
● skin becomes cold and clammy
● breathing and heart rate become rapid but weak
● the casualty may become drowsy or thirsty
● the casualty may lose consciousness.

To counteract shock, act immediately:
  1 Stop any bleeding (see above).
  2 Reassure and talk to the casualty.
  3 Lay the casualty down and raise the feet on a cushion.
  4 Keep the casualty warm and call an ambulance.

☐ Unconsciousness

  1 Shake the casualty gently and talk loudly to see if there is any response.
  2 Look for signs of breathing and if necessary give mouth-to-mouth ventilation.
  3 Search the body for broken bones, burns etc.
  4 Lay the casualty on his side and call for help.
  5 Never leave an unconscious person alone and never attempt to give food or drink.
  6 Even if the casualty appears to recover, he *must* see a doctor.

FIRST AID KIT

A first aid kit should contain the following:

● assorted waterproof adhesive dressings
● selection of sterile dressings
● gauze
● cotton wool
● selection of bandages
● porous surgical tape
● antiseptic wipes
● safety pin and scissors
● thermometer.

▲ *First Aid*

INDEX